MAKING
SENSE
OF
WINE

MAKING
SENSE
OF
WINE

Matt Kramer

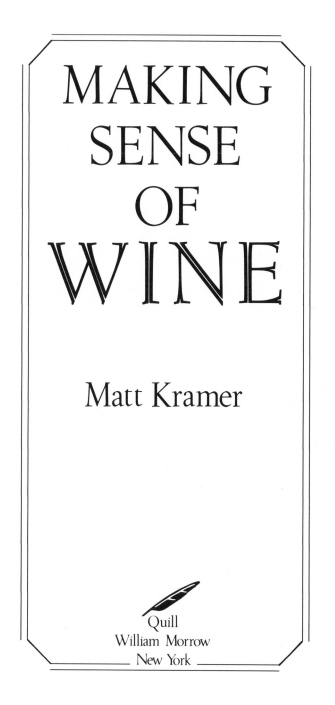

Quill
William Morrow
New York

Library of Congress Cataloging-in-Publication Data

Kramer, Matt.
    Making sense of wine / Matt Kramer — 1st ed.
        p.   cm.
    Includes index.
    ISBN 0-688-11917-4
    1. Wine and wine making. I. Title.
TP548.K678   1992
641.2′2—dc20   92-8219
                                                                         CIP

Printed in the United States of America

First Quill Edition

1 2 3 4 5 6 7 8 9 10

To the memory of William F. Cates, who taught me, and many others, that in life—as in wine—*sui generis* is the highest calling

Preface

Making Sense of Wine began in 1976, for that was the year I was faced with then-unwanted challenge of having to do just that. At the time (and still today) I had a great passion for food and cooking and had managed to change careers from bureaucrat to food editor for a weekly newspaper. My contract called for writing a lengthy food article and a restaurant review each week.

At the time I knew nothing of wine and had no intention of crossing its path. Wine seemed forbidding, snobbish, and, above all, daunting in its complication. I was suspicious of its trappings and cowed by its air of sophistication. I left it alone.

Before making the leap to food writing, my wife and I went bicycling in Europe for three months—another passion. She had been to Europe before, but it was my first time. Like so many others, my eyes were opened to ways of daily living, especially at the table, that I had never before experienced. Not surprisingly for a person with an intense interest in food, I was struck most of all by France and Italy.

Even so, I stoutly resisted the lure of wine, although we drank our daily liter of *vin ordinaire* every evening while sitting outside our tent, wondering if it could get any better than this. I now can answer that question: The wine, yes; the moment, no.

Anyway, after returning home I went to my new employer, the publisher of the weekly, who immediately asked what I knew about wine. I replied, honestly, that I knew that it came in red, white, and pink and with that he had exhausted my knowledge of wine.

It then was explained that while I was away the advertising department had prepared a mock-up of the new forthcoming food page and to fill up space had inserted an index. In that index they added a listing for something called Wine of the Week. Prospective advertisers liked the notion. I was to write it. "But I don't know anything about wine," I pleaded. "That's all right," replied the publisher. "Neither does anybody else."

This is how I came to wine. At best I was one sip ahead of some of my readers and gallons behind others. It was at that moment that I began to try to make sense of wine. Of course I read everything I could lay hands on which, even at that late date, was far less than exists in print now. In looking back, I now can see that I benefited greatly by having turned to some of the now-unread sages of the past such as P. Morton Shand, Cyrus Redding, James Busby, André Simon, Colette, and Henry Vizetelly, among others.

In addition, I went thousands of dollars into debt buying wines, a dozen bottles at a clip of red Bordeaux or California Chardonnays or Burgundies. How could I tell a reader that something was good if I hadn't any sense of the terrain? It was frightening, exhilarating, expensive, but above all, educational.

The most difficult part was gaining an understanding of what quality was all about. Like all wine novices, I first was attracted to size. Big, obvious wines seemed at the time to have the most to offer. Soon enough I recognized the need for restraint in wine, as my simultaneous involvement with food—where I did have some knowledge—demonstrated that these wines were louts at the table.

I also began to see that just having a command of the grammar of wine—specifics such as grape variety, label language, wine-making techno-talk—was insufficient. Learning how to read a wine label without learning why the information is significant is akin to learning a language without ever examining the culture it reflects, articulates, and defines. It is like being a tourist in a speeding, closed car. You see the place, but you have not *really* been there. I did not want to be a tourist of wine.

Making Sense of Wine reflects an ongoing search for the contexts that give meaning to wine and help make sense of something that is dizzying in its specifics and mystifying in its apparent lack of absolutes. I discovered that there are absolutes in wine, that not everything is merely a matter of taste. This is something only rarely acknowledged. In an egalitarian age, especially in American culture, it is bad form to suggest that what someone likes is not, *ipso facto*, good. But to make sense of wine requires a recognition and an acknowledgment of the values that make some wines better than others.

Making Sense of Wine is about why wine is so fundamentally satisfying, why its appeal crosses generational and cultural lines. That what we like today is what wine lovers in Regency England, Napoleonic France, Risorgimento Italy, Weimar Germany, and even ancient Greece also liked speaks volumes about the innate appeal of the best wines. Their qualities report directly to those underlying values—as opposed to the tastes—that make them so deeply and enduringly satisfying.

In this respect, wines are like dancers. No matter who is doing the judging, regardless of the culture, the age, or the choreography, great dancers always are recognized by the exhibition of the same values: control, line, grace, proportion, and fluidity, among others. So it is with wine, with its particular attributes.

Ultimately, the appeal of wine lies in its mystery. Of all agricultural endeavors, wine extracts something from the Earth that cannot quite be explained. Wines made from the same grape variety can taste different even when the vineyards are only a few hundred yards apart.

At first you look for technological answers and you find some.

One winemaker likes to store his wine in new oak barrels, which give the wine a particular scent and flavor. Another winemaker uses only stainless steel. One ferments the juice at a high temperature for a short time, while another prefers a lower temperature and a longer time. Each usually is convinced that his or her approach is the right one.

But after tasting a few wines, reading a few books, and talking to a few winemakers, it begins to dawn on you that there is no right answer. Winemakers today like to talk of "sculpting" a wine. They display their oak barrels, stainless steel tanks, and centrifuges and suggest, however indirectly, that these are what gives a wine its quality and appeal. Maybe it's so with grapes from second-rate sites.

But at their best, wine grapes have a way of giving voice to the Earth. Centuries ago someone gave Pinot Noir a try in Vosne-Romanée, Nebbiolo a chance in Barolo, and Chardonnay a shot in Chablis, and discovered not just a sweet evening plainsong, but a choral work of inspired complexity and cohesion. Yet just down the road, the same vine planted in a seemingly similar soil under an identical canopy of clouds and sun put forth only the simplest of chants.

This is the enduring, almost primordial appeal of great wines, the thing that allows our appreciation to span the generations: Wines express their source with exquisite definition. They allow us to eavesdrop on the murmurings of the Earth. Far from being composers, we really are just listeners.

Today our view of wine is increasingly mechanistic. Wines are judged like runners and scored accordingly. Nowadays it is not just fashionable, but considered plausible, to say that this wine rates an 89 while that wine deserves a 92. It makes wine seem a precise, manufactured substance that not only stands still long enough to be assigned an exact grade, but deserves one as well. This reflects the contemporary belief that in matters of taste everything is relative— and therefore competitive.

This approach does not let wine make sense. It just makes it orderly. Despite the fact that we have so many wines from which to choose, we do not need ever more pseudoprecise judgments about individual wines. We need a more fundamental understanding of what makes wines good. Only then can each of us sort through the array with any sense of security—or evaluate those who do so for us with such seeming exactitude.

Why does wine grip us? Perhaps because, far from being an answer, replete with a grade, wine is more a bottled question. The poet W. S. Merwin put his finger on it: *"The secret becomes no less itself for our presence in the midst of it. . . . Mystery is no more lucid for being near."*

Acknowledgments

The un-named rank and file miss their share of credit, as they must do, until they can write the despatches.

—T. E. Lawrence
The Seven Pillars of Wisdom

As the writer of this "despatch," I can only say that whatever the virtues of this book, I should like the following to get their share of credit. If, for some reason, they do not know what it is for I would be only too happy to give them a private accounting. As for whatever flaws lie herein, they had nothing to do with them. They are responsible only for their generosity and support.

Lalou Bize-Leroy, Ron Buel, Aldo Conterno, Armand Cottin, Louis Cottin, Bob Durst, Barbara Edelman, Maria Empson, Neil Empson, Bill Failing, Pierre-Henry Gagey, Angelo Gaja, Stephen Gilbertson, Maria Guarnaschelli, H. Stuart Harrison, Bill Hilliard, Karen Hinsdale, Ralph Kunkee, Greg Lemma, Aaron Millman, Ed Munves, Jr., Richard Olney, Peter Potterfield, Brian St. Pierre, Doreen Schmid, Vernon L. Singleton, John Tomsich, Bernard Trimbach, Hubert Trimbach, and above all others, my wife Karen.

Contents

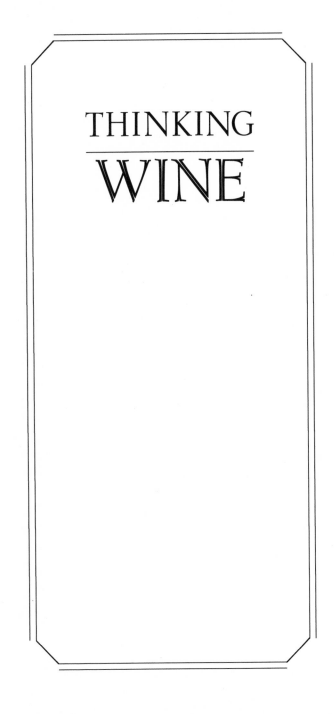

THINKING
WINE

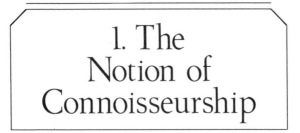

1. The Notion of Connoisseurship

One cannot know a country through geographical science alone . . . I don't believe that one can know anything through science alone. As an instrument, it is both too precise and too harsh. The world is filled with so many sorts of tenderness. To understand them, and before knowing what they represent as a whole, one must yield to them.

—Jean Giono
L'Eau Vive

Connoisseurship is a matter of attitude and approach. Perhaps to the surprise of some, knowledge is the least important element, although it is impossible to be a great connoisseur—what some people choose to describe as an expert—without a vast background in the subject at hand. Knowledge is easily enough acquired, at least for a reasonable degree of connoisseurship. But the mental posture that allows it to be collated and synthesized is not a mechanical process. A computer can never be a connoisseur.

One of the greatest connoisseurs I know is absolutely ignorant on the subject of wine. Yet he could become a first-rank wine connoisseur in as short a time as anyone humanly could should he so choose. Ed Munves, Jr., is well known in the rarefied circles of English antique silver. He owns James Robinson, Inc., a repository of exquisite (and expensive) antique silver and modern reproductions on East 57th Street in Manhattan.

My wife and I had made his acquaintance some years ago, in a first tentative foray in buying silver flatware. Ed spent hours chatting with us, a sure sign, as I look back now, of the connoisseur's unselfconscious enthusiasm for his subject. I doubt very much whether he thought for one moment that we were likely clients. But we were intrigued by his comments on the various qualities and authenticities of antique silver and by the quality of his reproduction flatware. The antiques were way out of our reach.

Several years later we got to know Ed a bit better and, as before, thoughts about authenticity and quality eased their way into the conversation. I believe we were examining silver coffeepots at the time. Ed motioned us into the *sanctum sanctorum* of James Robinson, a hushed, felt-lined private room housing the rarest and finest pieces in their possession. The three of us gazing upon gently lit shelves laden with venerable silver pieces must surely have looked like some religious gathering. Ed was like a kid in a mud puddle, though. I suspect that his feelings were not unlike some happy philatelist browsing through his stamp collection on a rainy Sunday afternoon. As we examined one pot or tray after another, Ed would offer a pithy, deeply informed précis on its previous owner, its significance historically or aesthetically, and its value.

"Sixty thousand dollars?" I found myself exclaiming.

"Yes," he answered evenly. "It is a lot, but you've got to remember just how rare it is. To a collector it's worth that."

"Well, what about you?" I inquired. "Is it worth that much to you?"

"I'm not a collector," he responded easily. "Let's face it, I don't want to be competing with my clients."

I asked him about the coffeepot he and his wife had in their home: Was it an original? "Actually it's not," he responded. "It's a reproduction of a rare pot that we once owned and eventually sold to a collector. We had our silversmiths make a reproduction of it—which is available to anyone—and that's the pot we use. We get a lot of pleasure out of it."

I felt that I was getting to the nub of things, at least to what was gnawing at me. "All right, I can understand why a museum or a wealthy collector would want the original, and would be willing to pay the price, but why should the rest of us be concerned whether something is an original or a splendid reproduction?"

"There's no reason at all," replied Ed. "There's ultimately nothing that makes something old superior to something new. But to a connoisseur of fine silver there is an indeterminable something that makes the original of something—old or new—distinctive. It's not a matter of patina or scratches or a dent. There is always something lacking in a reproduction, no matter how good a copy, that exists in an original. I guess you could say that it lacks the spontaneity of the hand that created it. An original reflects the mind and the hand of its creator. A reproduction can never capture this. You can see it, even if you can't quite explain its source.

"Let me tell you how I choose some of these items," he continued. "Typically there will be a private sale or an auction preview. I rarely go looking for something specific. All I'm looking for is quality, and in my case I'm looking for the absolute highest quality because that's our tiny slice of the market.

"Usually all the coffeepots, say, are lined up on a shelf. I don't think about anything; I suppose I just clear my mind. And I stand in front of the row of coffeepots and scan them, looking—just looking—at each one. I'm looking for something distinctive in the line of the pot. Or maybe there's an unusual aspect to a piece from a certain period that makes it stand out. Right away, in a matter of minutes, I usually eliminate most—sometimes all—of the pots. Then it gets down to two or three pots. No more. There are never very many pieces of the highest quality available at any one time.

"Then I draw closer and examine each piece further. I

look for any repairs that may have been done, anything that may make the piece inauthentic, any defects apart from the usual wear and tear of time and daily use.

"At that point my mind is pretty well made up as to its aesthetic and commercial worth, as well as how much I'm prepared to pay. The last thing I do is look at the hallmark, the individual brand of the maker. All this usually does is confirm what I suspected as to its origin and that can certainly affect my bid, although not my judgment of it. It's just a matter of the market at this point in the examination, which is a separate issue. Some silversmiths—Paul Revere, for example—always fetch a higher price because they are sought after for reasons of rarity, sentiment, or consistent quality. But really, the hallmark is just a means of setting a market value. However, if it's a lousy piece, I don't care who made it. And I won't buy it."

Why should anyone seek to be a connoisseur? Simply put, because it enhances one's pleasure, whether it be wine or automobiles or furniture. One can become a connoisseur of anything that offers gradations of quality.

When any of us is first exposed to something with any sort of complexity to it, our first reaction is the simplest: I like it/I don't like it. This is particularly persuasive with food and wine. After all, isn't the enjoyment of food and wine a matter of personal pleasure? It is, and there is absolutely no obligation for anyone to go beyond the blissful hedonism of that approach.

But the great appeal of wine, the thing that has sustained it as an object of unremitting attention from millions of people over hundreds of years is precisely that it offers us the opportunity to go beyond the bounds of I like it/I don't like it. At that moment, one enters into the realm of connoisseurship.

Unfortunately, the notion of connoisseurship is fraught with forbidding connotations, often of men with pointed goatees murmuring over glasses of wine about the intricacies of such and such a vintage compared to another. These folks exist—more in Hollywood than in real life—and they are just as offensive in reality as in conception.

In truth, connoisseurship is less a matter of what you know, and much more a matter of approach. As soon as one departs from the I like it/I don't like it platform, one has become something of a connoisseur. The simplest, and perhaps best, definition is that a connoisseur is one who can distinguish between what he or she likes, and what is good. The two are by no means always the same.

To be sure, there are levels of connoisseurship. A great connoisseur is a person with immense experience coupled with the connoisseur's approach. Experience alone isn't enough. I've met too many people who have tasted a great many bottles of wine—often very expensive wines—who are no connoisseurs at all. They know what they like and, typically, they evaluate the wine in hand using this standard: "I like Chateau Latour and this wine reminds me of Chateau Latour, *ergo* it is fine wine." The ideal connoisseur is actually someone who can say, after tasting a wine, "This is a great wine. But I can't stand it."

Inevitably, one comes to the essence of the matter: What constitutes quality in wine? How do you go about distinguishing between what tastes good to you and what is genuinely good? It's not as difficult as it may appear, nor is it as arbitrary as it sounds. In anything where matters of taste are important there is no one ideal, but there can be standards.

For example, the single greatest standard used in assessing the quality of a wine is complexity. The more times you can return to a glass of wine and find something different in it— in the bouquet, in the taste—the more complex the wine. The very greatest wines are not so much overpowering as they are seemingly limitless. One returns to the wine again and again, each time enlightened by a new sensation.

Complexity as a desideratum in fine wine is not an arbitrary standard. It appears that we are, in fact, set up to respond favorably to complexity. Decades of work in experimental psychology have revealed that when people are free to choose between a simple visual image and a more complex one, they gravitate to the complex. The same results obtain with simple and complex light patterns. These and other tests reveal that, over a period of time, we always seek more complex stimuli.

Even our alleged neurological compatriot, the laboratory rat, has demonstrated a preference, over time, for more complex stimuli over simple. In music, we invariably progress from the simple, or the "banal" as one researcher referred to nursery rhymes, to more complex melodic patterns.

What satisfies us so fundamentally about complexity is still the subject of speculation, largely in the academic field of aesthetics. It appears that we favor—relish might be a more descriptive, if less exact term—uncertainty or lack of predictability. One researcher contends that uncertainty in music *is* complexity. And that uncertainty gives greater "meaning" to music.

Another researcher in this field employs the notion of disorder or entropy. The more things are jumbled, the more "information" can be conveyed at one time. The trick is our ability to sort it out and make it meaningful. In short, there must be both pattern and uncertainty (complexity) for sustained interest. Complexity is thus more than multiplicity. For a wine (or a melody) to be truly satisfying, especially after repeated exposure, it must continually surprise us (uncertainty) and yet we must still be able to grasp these surprises as part of a larger and pleasing pattern. So it is with wine. For a wine to offer a kaleidoscope of flavors and aromas is not, in itself, enough. It's a start, certainly, but multiplicity of flavors and aromas without some sort of cohesion becomes jarring and eventually irritating.

Beyond complexity/uncertainty lie a number of less conspicuous and only somewhat less vital elements. A wine must have balance, for example. Balance, in wine terminology, is an equilibrium created by roughly equal amounts of "fruitiness" and acidity in wine. A wine that lacks fruit is said to be thin; if it is all fruit with no redeeming crispness—like an oversweet Rome apple rather than a Granny Smith—the wine is considered "flabby." The terminology is unimportant (except when you're trying to convey your thoughts to others), but the recognition is everything.

Balance in a wine is critical in that it makes a wine seem refreshing to us. The technically minded might say, "Can't you simply measure the level of acidity?" and the answer is yes. Enologists are forever referring to pH, malic acid, tartaric acid, titratable acidity, and so on. And we do know that below a certain level of acidity, a wine will very likely seem flabby to nearly all of us.

But recognizing whether or not a wine has balance can never be done in a laboratory. For balance is the interaction of acidity with the fruitiness of the wine (and sweetness in a sweet wine), and that interaction is not subject to the laws of physics and is not predictable. Moreover, our responses will differ somewhat from taster to taster, partly due to the fact that each of us has a slightly different physiological threshold for various substances, and partly due to experience. There is always a range in what constitutes balance both for every wine and for every person who drinks it. A wine, unlike a ballerina, is not either in balance or out.

In addition to balance and complexity, there is proportion, the equality or inequality of such aspects of a wine as bouquet, initial taste, middletaste, and aftertaste as they relate to each other. Good proportions are as self-evident in a wine as they are in a Hollywood starlet.

Enmeshed in all of these attributes is the even less precise concept of finesse. Of all the unquantifiable notions involved in connoisseurship, that of finesse is by far the most difficult to define. But it must be examined, as it is an essential in the achievement of the greatest quality for wines grown anywhere in the world.

Finesse is clearly a slightly Frenchified version of fineness, and that's as good a literal definition as any. But fineness fails to capture the nature of the quality implicit in a wine that has finesse. The concept of finesse, and the importance of it in a wine, is the result of an evolution in taste. It is far from a new notion, but it is more important now than ever before, as our technologically advanced wine-making skills have practically eliminated the chronic wine-making defects of the past, with the result that nearly all wines are at least palatable. The same skills have also allowed the better wines to appear deceptively fine, at least at first taste.

As with many things displaying gradations of quality, we tend to fashion for ourselves an ascending scale of greatness as we progress in our appreciation of wine. It is our way of making orderly sense out of the wonderful complexity/uncertainty of a flood tide of fine wines. Besides, it's terrific fun. Whatever scale is fashioned is at once stable—for we will always prefer the complex taste over the simple—and changeable, as new wines or winemakers come forward.

Yet what we value today differs markedly from what previous generations of wine lovers upheld as an ideal. A change in values often has to do with fashion, which itself can often be merely a response to rarity. But change or fashion in taste can just as easily be found in the desire for novelty or even a social need.

For example, the wines of the 1500s and 1600s, even those for the nobility, were coarse, cloudy in appearance, meant to be drunk within the year of the vintage, and were collectively indelicate. Not surprisingly, the most prized wines were those that were especially clear, light in body, and infused with a sapid delicacy. As William Younger in his scholarly *Gods, Men and Wine* explains, "Cloudy, discoloured, and evil smelling wines were a common disappointment of life." It is no wonder that, for the French court, the exquisitely fruity yet delicate wines of nearby Burgundy and Champagne—although vastly different then than now—were the most highly prized. The wines enjoyed by the French court in the 1500s and 1600s would likely fail to please us today even though the highest-quality wines may well have been beautifully made. By modern standards they were exceedingly light in weight and color, more frail and thin than what we would characterize today as delicate. They were meant to be drunk within a year of the vintage; the idea of a wine to be cellared was two centuries into the future. The French historian Fernand Braudel illustrates the point in *Civilization and Capitalism—The Structures of Everyday Life*: "In 1500 a cask of old Bordeaux cost only 6 livres tournois, while a cask of good new wine cost 50."

Yet our lack of appreciation for this style of wine may rest more with us than with the wine. It is difficult today to conjure up the emotional state of a past age and the appreciation of many wines does require a congenial state of mind. Modern practitioners of early music (Middle Ages and Renaissance) are uncomfortably aware of this fact. No matter how perfectionist they are in the construction of utterly authentic instruments and in the authentic method of playing them, there remains one insuperable hitch: The audience is listening with late-twentieth-century ears. We simply hear differently. We have forever lost a certain kind of acoustical innocence, with the result that early music, which seemed a rich tapestry to the fifteenth-century ear, in both the sound and the composition, can seem a little threadbare to us at least compared to the lush orchestration of the nineteenth century.

This desire for delicacy, at its most visually evident in a clear wine, is underscored by the evolution of the word *claret*. Today claret has a quite particular meaning, at least in Great Britain. There, claret is synonymous with the red wine of Bordeaux; a claret *is* a red Bordeaux.

But the origin of the word claret derives from the French *clairet*, clear. During the Middle Ages a *clairet* was a pure wine, light in color, which was often achieved by blending white wines with red wines—a rosé, in short. (The original red Bordeaux wines were very light in color, hence the evolution of *clairet* into claret.) Even as late as the seventeenth century, Champagne was still described as "claret and yellowish," the by-then modified word *claret* still referring to the clarity of the wine. It was high praise for a wine to be considered *clairet* or claret.

This also explains a minor mystery, namely, why the wine-making monk Dom Perignon wanted to create a sparkling Champagne. He worked at this task, successfully, from 1670 until he died in 1715. Yet why should he have wanted such a thing? After all, he wouldn't have known what a taste sensation it would be. The sparkling wines that did exist, largely by accident, were mere prickles in the mouth compared to the foaming effect he was seeking. What seems likely is that he was seeking to improve on the ideal of his day: clarity or limpidity in wine.

Dom Perignon was a fine enough winemaker to have already crafted a clear wine. And he was not modest about that accomplishment. A document in his own hand reveals that he considered the wine he made to be the *"meilleur vin du monde,"* the best wine in the world. What could be better than to emphasize the supreme clarity of his wine? And what could do that better than making it sparkle? After all, a cloudy wine with sparkling bubbles does nothing more than draw attention to that very defect.

But delicacy and clarity are not the criteria for finesse in contemporary wines. Where once the technology of wine making was so primitive that a clear wine was a rare creature (which is why old German wine glasses had colored cups, so as to hide the sediment and cloudiness of their white wines), today it is child's play to create a light, crystalline wine. It was also more than feasible a century ago.

Today our criteria for finesse are commingled with an appreciation for a great, clean, complex depth of flavor in a wine. But this appreciation emerged from yet another phase and another fashion. Where once delicacy was prized, sheer power became the next order of the day, this during the eighteenth century, most notably in England, but also in the Netherlands, Germany, and other northern European countries. The 1700s were the heyday of gin, brandy, alcoholic punches, and strong wines from Spain and Portugal. It was also the birthing century of that most powerful of wines, port, a strong, red wine from Portugal made even stronger (and easier to ship) by a bracing dose of brandy. Another fortified wine, Madeira, was already at its peak of popularity. It was a time of drunkenness and monumental benders unequalled before or since, at every level of society. (The French and the Italians, perhaps because they produced such fine wines, appear to have avoided these excesses.) The English aristocracy, reputed to buy only the best from France, paid extra and dearly for a wine as fine as Château Lafite—already highly regarded—to be blended with Hermitage, a deeply colored, strong red wine of the Rhône Valley. This practice obtained well into the 1800s as a stated and preferential procedure. Such blending for strength and color, in both red Bordeaux and red Burgundy, continues surreptitiously to this day. The practice is increasingly rare, however.

This preference for power and strength in wine was, it might be noted, of a piece with the musical desires of the age as well. The late 1700s and early 1800s saw the rise of the Romantic movement. Not only were concert halls enlarged, but new and louder musical instruments replaced the too-soft, too insipid-sounding (to contemporary ears) instrumentation of an earlier age. Composers developed new arrangements of sound to answer the new social need. As one musical scholar of the period, Raymond Leppard, observes, "Everything had to be louder, brighter, faster."

Nevertheless, connoisseurship of wines continued to increase dramatically. The lust for power in wine eventually yielded to a recognition that power without subtlety, depth of flavor without balance, color without underlying substance were unrewarding. At this imprecise point in time—starting roughly in the 1860s—the concept of finesse as we know it today began to make itself felt.

At present, a wine with finesse can be said to be one that has achieved a particularly striking harmony of its parts. One is tempted to rummage around in the Oriental stockpile of words to describe such oneness. Precisely because this integrity is so inexact, it is quite impossible to define.

Wines at all levels of strength and weight can achieve finesse. In fact, it is most easily achieved by white wines, especially the more delicate ones such as Rieslings from the Rheingau and Mosel valleys of Germany. But this business of finesse is much more prized—and more difficult to achieve—in richer, stronger wines. And when wines do achieve it, they are considered correspondingly greater. The greatness of rich, strong white wines such as Le Montrachet or Meursault "Perrières," both Chardonnays from Burgundy, is that they manage to be powerful yet graceful. They have finesse.

This is at its most striking in the great red wines. The forces brought to bear by the sheer depth of fruit, tannin, and complexity of flavors found in a fine red wine make the achievement of finesse that much more difficult. The lighter red wines display it more readily, such as the red wines of Graves for example, or some of the medium-weight Pinot Noirs from Burgundy or Oregon.

But when one enters into the realm of great Cabernet Sauvignons, Merlots, or Nebbiolos, finesse is rare indeed. Only the finest among Barolos and Barbarescos, California Cabernets, and red Bordeaux can pull it off, and our fascination with such wines is that much greater. It is not unlike the unique appeal of certain heavyweight fighters. Joe Louis, for instance, was hardly a pugilist of finesse. Power, strength, endurance, yes; but he lacked finesse. Muhammad Ali, on the other hand, was a heavyweight fighter of great finesse. He handled himself with the speed and precision of a lightweight boxer, yet he packed the power and the punch of a heavyweight. One expects speed, ease of movement, and deftness from a lightweight, but from a heavyweight it is a rare form of harmony, a conciliation of distinctly separate traits. It is compelling. A wine that lacks finesse can certainly be considered good, but rarely is it among the handful of greats. Such accolades are, however, a matter of taste and fashion. A society slogging through a protracted war or a prolonged depression, such as when Joe Louis fought, may well value the virtue of sheer endurance and doggedness over agile footwork. The popularity or acclaim for certain styles or types of wine can be the mirror of an age.

How future historians will characterize our particular moment in the long span of wine loving is impossible to predict. Certain characteristics, however, will doubtless be highlighted. Ours is an age of enormous scientific advances in wine, in the technology of its manufacture, in understanding its chemistry and organic mysteries, and in redefining the received—and often erroneous—wisdom of centuries of un-scientific, superstitious wine tradition.

This ascendancy of science in wine making has taken its toll on a new generation of wine lovers, especially American wine lovers. Having no long-standing tradition of wine drinking in this country, and much respect for the scientific way, an enormous number of brand-new wine drinkers have had their tastes and standards shaped by this new, decidedly un-romantic, technical vision of quality in wine.

Wine tasters in America can talk more like winemakers than connoisseurs. The technology of wine making has become, for many aficionados, more important than what results from it. It serves to define rather than simply to serve. (We can see a similar insinuation in the spread of the computer and its methodology.) Future historians will likely note this as a passing phase, at least one hopes so. As Jean Giono so eloquently observes, science is both too precise and too harsh an instrument. It is no longer enough, as it was for the great André Simon in the earlier part of this century, that a connoisseur be someone who is able to recognize the authentic in wine. His was an era of blatant fraud and abuse in the making and labeling of wine. Our more legally regulated and scientifically astute time has eliminated the great bulk of such malpractice, although the ability to recognize the authentic in wine will always be needed.

Today, the connoisseur has the quite subtle and demanding challenge of being able to distinguish between the technically good and the genuinely fine in wines, in more wines than even the far-seeing André Simon could have envisioned. The world is awash with new wines from comparatively new or revived wine-growing regions: the Pacific Northwest, California, New York State, New Zealand, Australia, Romania, Chile, Yugoslavia, and at least a dozen other promising locales. By the technical standards of the day many of these wines, even most, are good. They are free of wine-making defects, filled with a fresh-tasting fruit, and sometimes promising of even more than that. But how fine are they?

Here the enologists and their "too precise and too harsh" scientific vocabulary must give way to the less quantifiable, the less provable notions of connoisseurship. The role of the connoisseur cannot be usurped by science, nor intimidated by it.

By the same measure, the connoisseur must yield freely to the fact that greatness is not just the province of a few time-honored plots of land in Bordeaux or Burgundy, or that other wines must replicate these established reference points in order to achieve equal claim to greatness. The wine lover's sole responsibility is to entertain herself or himself in a pastime that has amused generations before us: to cheerfully peruse the offerings, attempting to distinguish the great from the good, quality from mere preference.

2. Wine in the Cellar and Society

Every carving, every mask, served a specific religious purpose, and could only be made once. Copies were copies; there was no magical feeling or power in them; and in such copies Father Huismans was not interested. He looked in masks and carvings for a religious quality; without that quality the things were dead and without beauty.

—V. S. Naipaul
A Bend in the River

The two most pressing questions that beset the wine lover are: Which wines should I buy? And when will they be ready to drink? The first question is the easier to answer, despite the proliferation of wines. Any number of private wine newsletters, to say nothing of newspaper and magazine articles, endeavor to keep the wine-interested abreast of the latest releases and their relative quality. There's no murk in this matter.

But when to drink is something else again. Here advice-givers become vague: "Ready to drink in two to five years" or "Drink now to 2001," which is a big help. Such indefinite advice reveals the problem of when to drink: Too much depends upon your personal taste. Added to this are such variables as the manner in which the wine has been stored and the nature of the wine itself. Do you prefer wines when they are young and fruity? Or are the characteristics of well-aged wines more to your liking?

The idea of an aged wine being inherently superior is so much a part of the transgenerational vision of fine wine that there is little sense in trying to dislodge it. For the record, age does not make a wine better. It can make it more accessible. Or smoother. Or rounder. It can go down the gullet with less of a catch. Old wines can have the *characteristics* of age, but not necessarily the character.

Actually, it is a misnomer to talk about fine wines aging. The best wines do not age so much as they transform. This is the signature of all ageworthy wines. It is the reason why one cellars a wine and why certain wines require extended time in the bottle. It also is the reason why wine connoisseurs can sometimes seem so all-fired sure about when a wine is *not* ready to be drunk: What they are sure of is that the transformation is not likely to have yet taken place. Before that moment, you are drinking promise rather than achievement, like fishing for steelhead while they are still rainbow trout.

An example of this is Chablis, the 100 percent Chardonnay wine from the Chablis district of France. To taste a young Chablis, especially a *premier* or *grand cru*, is to fail to see what all the accolades are about. When two, three, or even four years old they seem tart, tight, and ungenerous. Pleasure, let alone depth of character, is difficult to find. The classic description of a rich stony or minerally quality coupled with a profound depth rivaling some of the other great white Burgundies seems absent. One wonders what the hoopla is about. Yet when this same Chablis reaches the age of between five and ten years old—it depends on the vintage—the wine transforms. With Chablis the transformation is extreme, on the order of the caterpillar to the butterfly.

This is not to say that all fine wines need age. The great Moscato wines from the Asti district of Piedmont can be magnificent, yet youthful freshness is essential. The same is true for the red Dolcetto wines of the same area, as well as *fino* sherries from Spain, most Beaujolais, and all but the best sparkling wines, including French Champagnes.

In some instances, such as Cabernet Sauvignon, the need for aging is readily apparent, although the amount of age needed for transformation can vary dramatically. Here the experts can only hedge their bets. Wines, like children, don't always turn out as fine as one hopes—or as bad as one fears. Other wines, for example the great Chenin Blancs from the Loire Valley such as Savennières, the best Vouvray, Quarts de Chaume, or Bonnezeaux, give not even a wink of encouragement as to forthcoming charms. The same is true for German Riesling, which hides its luminosity of flavor under bushels of youthful acidity.

Among red wines, Nebbiolos from the Piedmont region of northwestern Italy always transform. Barolo and Barbaresco, each 100 percent Nebbiolo, require the better part of a decade to reveal the exceptional complexity of the wine. More deceptive is Pinot Noir, which is much more approachable and enjoyable when young. Yet the best red Burgundies such as Mazi-Chambertin from Leroy, Bonnes-Mares from Domaine Georges Roumier, or even a silky wine such as Volnay "Clos des Ducs" from the Marquis d'Angerville, call for years in the bottle before the grandness of these wines erupts in a cloud of perfumes. Here the expectation of transformation is less obvious because these wines taste awfully good when young. Who could be blamed for figuring that it doesn't get any better than this?

On the other hand, some seemingly fine wines never transform, or do so only reluctantly and to no distinctive end. An example of this is the Tempranillo grape of Spain, also known as Ull de Llebre. A genuinely good grape that creates some of the best red wines of Spain, it creates long-lived wines. More than most grapes, Tempranillo resists oxidation. So it is possible to taste old Tempranillo wines that display a wondrous freshness. Tasting a young one you are impressed: The wine seems to have real possibilities. With age, you surmise, this will become something really fine. And so you wait and wait and then wait some more. But even after twenty years of aging, all you discover is the same (appealing) taste you found earlier, smoother and rounder, but the same. It does not transform. It only endures, polished by time like a promising stone given lapidary care only to reveal no great depth or brilliance. This is the difference between maturation and transformation.

What goes on inside the bottle that such transformations can occur? The answer begins with Louis Pasteur, who, at the request of Napoleon III in 1863, investigated the causes of the deterioration of wine. Pasteur discovered that oxygen was the culprit. Wines exposed to air (which is 21 percent oxygen) went bad because of the growth of vinegar bacteria. His investigation did not stop there. Intrigued by the role played by oxygen in the aging of wine, Pasteur set up a series of experiments in which red and white wines were placed in test tubes. One test tube was completely filled with red wine and one with white and then sealed to prevent any air from entering. The others were only half-filled with red wine or white and then sealed, which left air inside.

By this simple but effective method Pasteur was able to show a dramatic difference in color in both the red and white wines. The completely filled test tubes showed no change in color after several weeks. But the half-filled test tubes, red and white, were badly deteriorated, both showing the brown hue that characterizes very old wines. With this, Pasteur pointed out the profound role played by oxygen in the aging process.

Technically, the browning does not result from oxidation, which is the absorption of oxygen into the wine, resulting in a flat, off taste and smell caused by the presence of aldehydes, which are chemical compounds created when the alcohol absorbs oxygen. Instead, the browning results from enzymatic oxidation, which occurs when enzymes in the wine combine the oxygen with the tannins and pigments, resulting in browning. Unlike oxidation, it does not change the flavor. A good example of this is a cut apple left exposed. It quickly browns, but the flavor remains unchanged. Since the two processes often appear together, the distinction between oxidation proper and enzymatic oxidation are blurred and usually ignored except by wine technicians.

When a red wine ages, its color changes from a bright purplish ruby to a ruby garnet. From there it takes on orange and brown tinges and progressively pales, reaching what some observers call a tile color. Eventually it becomes outright brown, at which point the wine is shot. The color comes from two sources: tannins, which stabilize color, and the color agents themselves, called anthocyanins. These are the red, blue, and purple pigments found in the grape skins of red wine grapes. White wine grapes have a different set of anthocyanins. Under the influence of oxygen, the tannins and anythocyanins combine, which over time results in color changes.

This dual responsibility for color explains two phenomena that have long baffled observers about red wines. One is the fact that a very young, vibrantly colored red wine can lose color. The other, even more baffling, is that a light-colored wine can *gain* color. What happens in the first instance is that the highly colored wine has more anthocyanins than tannins. The oxygen, not being bound up by the tannins, has its oxidative way with the anthocyanins, with the result that some of the coloring matter is lost.

In the instance of a wine gaining color with age—this happens with some Pinot Noirs—the wine has relatively few anthocyanins compared to tannins. Over time, the two elements combine, creating a deeper color than when they were acting separately. This is more common in Pinot Noir because the grape variety lacks certain anthocyanins commonly found in other red wine grapes, resulting in initially paler wines than Merlot or Cabernet Sauvignon, for example.

Color aside, the relationship between wine and oxygen is, to use psychological jargon, conflicted. Wine both is in need of and undone by oxygen. It needs it during its early upbringing, which is why so many wines, red and white, are still aged in wood barrels in which a slight amount of air insinuates itself into the wine. This does not happen, as is commonly thought, from the porosity of the wood. According to Professor Emile Peynaud in *Knowing and Making Wine* (1981), experiments have demonstrated that the penetration of oxygen through the staves of an oak cask is on the order of two to five milliliters of oxygen per liter of wine a year, depending upon the thickness and type of wood. Large oak casks whose staves are two inches thick admit virtually no oxygen at all.

Instead, oxygen comes from three sources: the headspace found in nearly every barrel or cask; the topping-up procedure, when a barrel or cask is opened and the evaporated wine replenished; and racking, in which a wine is siphoned from its sediment into a clean barrel. Topping up is a weekly procedure; racking occurs six to eight times before a wine is bottled. Although excess exposure to air in these processes is harmful, a brief encounter is considered stimulating.

The conflict is in the different needs of the wine in barrel and bottle. Wine in the barrel benefits from a slight exposure to air. Yet wine in the bottle is undone by it. Contrary to common belief, wine receives no significant additional oxygen once it is bottled and sealed. It is true that some oxygen contained within the cork itself—its cells are miniature shock absorbers holding oxygen and nitrogen—is released into the wine after corking. This release amounts to a few tenths of a cubic centimeter of oxygen, which is as much a tribute to modern abilities to measure minute quantities than anything else. Afterward, according to Peynaud, the amount of oxygen that slips past the sides of the cork is "insignificant, representing a few hundredths of a cubic centimeter. Therefore," he concludes, "[free] oxygen could never be an agent in bottle aging."

So what happens when a wine matures in an airtight, oxygen-free environment, i.e., a tightly corked bottle? The generally accepted theory is called reduction or redox reaction. To the scientific mind, oxidation is not a matter of a gloriously red or white wine turning brown. That's just a symptom. Instead, oxidation is a matter of a molecular loss (reduction) or gain (oxidation) of hydrogen or electrons, hence RED(uction)OX(idation). These shuttle back and forth in the wine, causing chemical reactions. Like a well-executed equation, whenever one substance loses something, another gains. Thus various alcohols, sugars, and acids in the wine are chemically altering, resulting in the formation of yet other substances, such as esters, that create the subtle scents that come with bottle age. All of this occurs in the absence of oxygen. Yet it could not have happened as effectively if the wine had not been exposed to small amounts of it earlier on. A wine kept hermetically sealed from the day its fermentation is complete never matures to as good, or even comparable, an end as one that has seen some oxygen before being shut in.

This is the science of wine aging. Reassuring as it sounds, it doesn't tell us much. For example, we have no idea why Château Lafite-Rothschild comes out tasting as delicate and ethereal as it does after fifteen or twenty years while another wine of similar origins and structure comes to no good end— or just a different end—after the same length of time. What goes on in the bottle is just too complex to be unraveled, let alone traced. For all its high-sounding phrases, the science of wine aging so far is little more than dogged detective work that remains far from solving the crime, however promising the clues. The painter Matisse captured its limitations: *"L'exactitude ce n'est pas la vérité"* (Precision is not truth).

All of which leaves the wine lover back where it all happens anyway, namely, in the cellar watching one's wines grow up. In this regard, we have become impatient. Our idea of time has contracted radically from that of our grandparents. The wines we drink today reflect this: They are made to mature sooner. This is nothing to lament. Increasingly, though, modern wines are also made to taste good right out of the starting gate, which in some instances comes at the expense of greatness later on, a sort of borrowing for today's Peter at the expense of tomorrow's Paul.

Today's taste in wine, regardless of color or type, is for

young and fruity. Witness the astonishing success of Beaujolais Nouveau, a 100 percent Gamay wine from the Beaujolais region of France that is released in mid-November, only weeks after it finishes its fermentation. You can't beat it for being vibrantly fresh and fruity. Today, fully half of the production of the Beaujolais region is sold as *nouveau*, roughly eight million cases a year, where once it was just a local oddity.

Although Beaujolais Nouveau is modern and dramatic testimony to the taste for young and fruity, the fact is that this taste has been a long time coming. It dates to just after World War I. The stocks of wines on the Continent and in Britain were virtually exhausted between 1914 and 1918, as resupply from the ravaged fields of France—where at the time all the truly fine wine originated—was impossible. Existing French stocks were commandeered by the German occupiers, who appropriated not only the fine wines but the crude daily tipple as well, which they converted into industrial alcohol. They did the same in World War II. Although America was a small factor in the world appreciation of fine wine, it, too, exhausted its stocks of wines and wiped out its wineries, courtesy of Prohibition, which lasted from 1919 to 1933. Between these two events, the stage was set for a permanent alteration in preferred tastes in wine.

The cause of the change was first necessity, then fashion. With stocks of old wines depleted, there was no choice but to drink wines that would previously have been considered barbarously young. Not least, World War I profoundly changed the social structure of Europe. An increasing number of the formerly wealthy were now merely affluent, if that. Housing was in short supply and for the first time, large numbers of people lived in apartments, few of which offered a proper cellar for wine storage. P. Morton Shand, an upper-class English writer of the old school (born 1888), captures the effect of this change in housing when he recalls in the revised edition of *A Book of French Wines* (1960), "The arrival of unexpected guests often compelled a host to send out for wine, which his parents would have considered the acme of domestic ignominy."

The stately, stodgy fussiness of pre–World War I living was thrown over with a vengeance. Cocktails were the rage and young wines replaced the cobwebbed bottles of an era seen, even then, as forever gone. The 1920s, as later in the 1960s, saw an all-cleansing virtue in youth.

Despite this, the finest wines changed only very slowly, if at all, until the late sixties. Partly this was due to the natural conservatism of winegrowers, who, like farmers everywhere, are reluctant to throw over old ways. But partly it was due to the slow accumulation and even slower transmission of scientific knowledge of wine. With it came control, which now is pursued and practiced zealously. Where technique was once a haphazard and largely intuitive thing, now winemakers in California talk about "sculpting" a wine.

Chablis, once again, is a convenient example. Old wine books habitually suggest that a good Chablis is not drinkable until ten years after the vintage and a great Chablis, a *premier* or *grand cru*, needs fifteen or twenty years to be fully drinkable. As late as 1935, the London wine merchant Charles Walter Berry in his book *In Search of Wine—A Tour of the Vineyards of France* advised about Chablis: "Do not keep the fine wines of 1900, 1904 and 1906, but drink them while they are so excellent."

Few Chablis today offer such longevity. This is not the same, however, as saying that they are not as good. Longevity and quality are not synonymous, however tempting the idea. The difference lies in the fact that prior to World War II, the wines of Chablis did not typically undergo a malolactic fermentation. This process, which also is known as a secondary fermentation, is caused not by yeasts but by bacteria. Where in the first, or primary, fermentation yeasts convert the sugar in the grape juice into alcohol, thereby creating the wine, in the secondary or malolactic fermentation bacteria convert the harsh malic acid in the wine into softer lactic acid. The result is an overall decrease in acidity and a softening of the wine, which can be desirable in high-acid wines such as Chablis.

This practice of intentionally putting the wines through a malolactic fermentation is new. Although it occurs naturally, winemakers had no knowledge of what actually was going on and thus no control. They couldn't initiate the process nor, if they wanted, stop it if it began. Cold prevents the process from starting, and since the cellars of Chablis are always cold, the old Chablis wines retained all of their original, harsh acidity. The wines were undrinkable for years until this acidity mellowed. On the other hand, such high acidity is immensely effective in preserving a wine. But even now, with malolactic fermentation a universal practice in the district (they heat the cellars to get it going), Chablis still remains a wine that demands five to ten years for its beauty to unfurl.

Most fine wines today undergo malolactic fermentations, but a few do not because it would be to the detriment of the wine style, especially in the case of sweeter wines. The best example of this is German Rieslings, which often contain significant amounts of residual sugar. Without a compensatory amount of acidity, the wines would taste cloying rather than rich. Moreover, we wouldn't find them refreshing to drink, as they would taste as flat and lifeless as fruity sugar water. Instead they are an exciting balancing act between fruitiness, sweetness, and zingy acidity. To achieve this, German winegrowers need to retain acidity—at least in the best vintages—rather than reduce it, with the result that the richer German Rieslings do not undergo a malolactic fermentation. The benefit is that these wines are not only brilliantly balanced, but are among the most long-lived of all modern wines. The drawback is that they frequently are unpleasant when young, say three or four years old. But after that, the acidity softens, the fruit emerges, and what once seemed harsh and schizoid—sweet clashing with acid—suddenly emerges as harmonious.

All of which brings us back to that overriding question: When is a wine ready to drink? Transformation aside, the answer is that it rests as much with the drinker as the wine. It is a matter of attitude. Much of the underlying pressure of the question comes from a misleading vision of wine, namely that wines reach a "peak". Although both the term and the notion are used innocently, this business of a peak is a disservice both to drinkers and to wine itself. There is no peak. As long as one continues to think about when a wine will "reach its peak," insecurity and doubt will grow at the expense of pleasure and insight.

The idea of a wine reaching its peak is narcotically appealing. You taste a young wine that clearly needs more age and you know, regardless of inexperience or taste, that the wine is not yet ready to drink. So you say, without a moment's hesitation, "It needs a few years to reach its peak." The phrase seems innocent.

But language is not innocent. Indeed, language shapes thought and this is just such an instance. As soon as we envision a peak, inevitably we see an up side and a down side. At the apex is, naturally, the fabled peak. It suggests an all-too-brief moment of glory, one moment only. The height is scaled only to descend from a pinnacle of perfection.

Many wine drinkers, recoiling from this illegitimate vision, instead suggest that the maturation of a wine more resembles a plateau than a peak. They see a bell curve, where a young wine starts out at the base of the curve and, as it matures, gradually traces an upward path that eventually flattens into a plateau. The line then slants down, the steepness of its descent depending upon the taster's notion of how rapidly the wine goes off form. Great red Bordeaux, for example, usually are seen as having a generous plateau and a long, gradual slope on the downside. Beaujolais, on the other hand, are seen with a sharply accelerating maturation curve upward, like a Cobra 427 going from zero to 100. It enjoys a brief flattening out at the top and then skids downward in an equally abrupt decline.

This bell curve vision is reassuring, as it seems to address the slipperiness of the notion of wine having a peak. Still, it fails to satisfy because it is mere palmistry, tracing a lifeline that is more a generalized and reassuring illusion than a particular reality. So it is between a wine and its drinker. Far from slogging up or sliding down, the life of a wine is more a continuum. There is no moment when a wine is at its best.

There is a birth, an adolescence, a maturity, and eventually a death. But along that lifeline, as along our own, is there really one moment and only one when the wine is absolutely best? I, for one, would not like to assume that I won't have desirable qualities at seventy or, for that matter, that I didn't have certain attractions at seventeen. When I was (or will be) at my best is mercifully a matter of the taste of the beholder.

Cellaring wine is like wanting children. If you like children, which, as with wine, is a reasonable prerequisite, it's doubtful that you want them simply because of how wonderful they'll be when they reach eighteen or thirty-two or any other age. Presumably, one has them for the pleasure of watching them grow up, of enjoying their company along the way and partaking of the pleasures that each level of maturity brings with it. So it is with wine. "Who can say that this one here is better than that one there?" asks Lalou Bize-Leroy, co-owner of the Domaine de la Romanée-Conti. "Each one is different. At the moment of bottling, a new life begins."

This brings us to a blunt practicality: If the pleasure of wine is in watching it grow up, then a bottle or two won't do the trick. This is the difference between tasting and connoisseurship. Until one has watched a wine evolve, has sampled it with various dishes, good and bad, and has decided for oneself at what point along the continuum of the wine's life one most enjoys its company, a wine is no more meaningful than a song heard once over the car radio.

In the case of wine, it takes just that: A case of a dozen bottles. Only when you buy by the case can you amass enough of a wine to have the pleasure of watching it grow up. Too often, wine drinkers are excited by the reports of high-priced wines that are the regular fare of wine publications. To read these reports, there are wines out there that are transports of delight. You must try them, be they Château Lafite-Rothschild or Le Montrachet or the latest fifty-dollar wonder from California. And so the wine drinker of limited means buys one bottle, perhaps two, and hurries home with visions of vinous sugarplums dancing in his or her head.

You know what happens next. Because most of us have limited wine cellars, at best, it's impossible to forget about this jewel that very nearly glows in the dark every time you pass by your wine hoard. And you know, if only because the books say so, that the wine should be aged. You wonder, "When will it be ready to drink?" Also, it becomes increasingly hard to forget just how expensive it was and, after a few years, how much more it's worth now. Soon the wine takes on a totemic quality. It becomes a fetish, an object of devotion and anticipation that no wine, no matter how wonderful, could ever fulfill. This is not wine loving. Maybe it's collecting or worship or simply feeling like you're with it. But it's not wine loving.

So what is this high-sounding thing called wine loving? It's living with wines. It's buying what you can afford to drink—psychologically as well as financially. A good rule of thumb when the sirens tempt is: If you can't afford a case of it, you can't afford it—well, six bottles anyway. This may seem severe, but wine today has become too precious, in both senses of the word. And this preciousness has already exacted a price.

The price has been a scuttling toward safety, toward a sameness in what we drink. The result has been what might be called a franchising of wine. The notion of franchising in this instance is not understood completely in a narrow business sense, in which one successful operation is cloned to become one thousand such operations, although this is part of what franchising is all about. Instead, franchising here reflects a larger societal impulse toward predictability, reliability, and, above all, security. This liking for the franchised is shaping our choices due to something perhaps not always acknowledged: *They* are not franchising us; *we* are franchising them.

The result of this desire to franchise taste is not merely a protection against unpleasant surprises. As in learning a foreign language, but refusing to brave a chat with a native, you end up having the same conversation over and over again. Individuality and variety are being stifled. An unwillingness to pursue and celebrate individuality threatens to erode what might be called the ecology of wine. As in a rain forest or a coral reef, what makes wine so fascinating is its variety. This has been impinged upon, not just in terms of the grape varieties planted, but in how the message of the wine itself is being transmitted. The variety that is the eternal fascination of wine will not be so easily found, or be as authentic as one might think, much in the same way as asking a national park to accommodate Winnebagos and yet thinking that it still is wilderness.

For example, American wine drinkers have so far chosen to franchise just two grape varieties: Cabernet Sauvignon for red wine and Chardonnay for white. As merchants across the nation will confirm, woe unto the red or white wine that isn't composed of one or the other. It will have a tough vineyard row to hoe. The result has been an outsized emphasis on these two grape varieties worldwide, partly because the American influence in wine making and grape growing now is ascendant, but also because the American taste in wine reflects something larger. The Americanization of wine is occuring even in long-established wine-growing nations because they share, perhaps more than is realized, the same revolution in wine consumption that is taking place now in the United States, namely, the emergence of an enormous number of wine drinkers who are new to fine wine. It is true even for such wine-besotted countries as France and Italy, as well as Switzerland, Belgium, the Netherlands, and Germany. Although wine has long been a beverage for most Europeans, it was not something to which most drinkers gave any thought, largely because the daily tipple didn't deserve it. The more profound wines that do encourage reflection were financially out of reach or were considered socially inappropriate. In Piedmont, for example, where Barolo reigns supreme, a worker who liked wine would lay down on the birth of a son not Barolo, but Barbera. It was the peasant's grape, and Barolo was far above his sense of station, as well as more expensive.

With the expansion of Western economies in the 1960s,

1970s, and 1980s, and the great distribution of wealth that resulted, an enormous number of drinkers new to fine wine, or to wine at all, have reshaped the modern taste. They are, by far, the biggest demand group. Not having had the benefit of tasting mature wines nor the luxury of being personally tutored in wine as was the privilege of long-ago aristocrats, the new drinkers are on their own. They want two things from their wines: a taste that can be readily identified and something immediately accessible. Prevailing fashion dictates that it should be dry rather than sweet.

The need for easy identification of taste and accessibility makes sense. Learning about wine is like learning a foreign language. As anyone who has struggled through a foreign language can attest, the most gratifying moment is when, after months of unrewarding, seemingly useless effort, you suddenly understand what someone is saying. You may not get it all, but you get the gist. And when you respond, they understand you. You are communicating, and it is wonderful.

So it is with newcomers to wine. For those for whom wine is a brand-new taste, wine is as baffling as a new language and only a little more pleasurable. In this context the appeal of Cabernet Sauvignon is that no red grape variety has a more easily identifiable and pleasurable taste. It shows itself clearly no matter where the grape is grown, be it Romania, Bordeaux, Tuscany, or Napa Valley. No dialect is beyond you if the language is Cabernet. Among the white wines—keeping in mind that dry is paramount—no grape variety has more obvious charms than Chardonnay. Equally as important, both grapes have unassailable pedigrees, respectively Bordeaux and Burgundy. Also—more about this later—both varieties are aged in small oak barrels, which give drinkers another clue.

The result has been a rise not just of varietal names for wines, with the name of the grape supplanting that of a place, but of a varietal orientation in the flavor of wines. This is the more long-term influence of the tidal wave of new drinkers. The most obvious effect of this is the intrusion of Cabernet Sauvignon and Chardonnay into districts that never before cultivated these varieties. These are the two grapes that attract the greatest attention, price, and praise, so they get planted. In the Piedmont region of northwestern Italy, where Nebbiolo creates Barolo and Barbaresco, you now find new plantings of Cabernet Sauvignon and, especially, Chardonnay. Farther south, in Tuscany, where Sangiovese is indigenous, the craze is for Cabernet Sauvignon. In Australia, where for centuries the Shiraz, or Syrah, grape has created that country's most memorable red wine, it has been spurned in favor of the glamour of Cabernet. The same is happening in Spain and, of course, in various regions of the United States, where the trend toward varietalness, in both name and taste, first began.

The problem is not a matter of keeping everyone in his place. Experimentation is at the heart of winegrowing. After all, Burgundy and Bordeaux, Piedmont and Napa Valley were not preordained only for those grapes that are their signatures. Instead, the problem is that, increasingly, a grape variety must be franchised in order to secure a market. And that franchise is identifiable varietalness.

This has extended itself to the much more subtle but critical issue of clonal selection. Clones are strains of a plant. Grapevines are genetically unstable. If grown from seed, the chances are good that they will not reproduce truly from the mother plant. Over the centuries, grapevines have been reproduced in the same way that my grandmother reproduced her African violets, by cloning—taking a stem and rooting it until it became a thriving plant in its own right. This has led to a multiplicity of clones within a variety, often within the same vineyard. Pinot Noir is the most extreme example, with over two hundred clones identified, but most varieties display ten or twenty clonal variations should anybody care to sort through them.

Clonal differences can be minor and major. Individual berries can be tiny or unusually large. The yield can be grudging or enthusiastic. The color can be intense or pale. The foliage can be abundant or sparse. The vine can be delicate or robust. The resulting wine can be dark in color or unusually fragrant or have one particular quality, perhaps a pronounced scent, that sets it apart. Many observers contend that a mixture of clones in a vineyard is far superior to just one or two.

Starting in the 1960s, both American and European researchers began to isolate and catalog clones of various grape varieties, notably for Pinot Noir and Chardonnay. In California, Professor Harold P. Olmo of the University of California at Davis Department of Viticulture and Enology performed numerous trials with various clones of Chardonnay and Cabernet Sauvignon. In the case of Chardonnay, he eventually selected and recommended for wide-scale reproduction a handful of clones that consistently passed trials for yield, disease resistance, and flavor. It is widely thought that the quality of California Chardonnays increased dramatically as a result of his efforts in isolating the better clones for California growers. An even larger effort to do the same for Cabernet Sauvignon proved less fruitful. According to Olmo, "We didn't come out with very much in Cabernet Sauvignon because we had some very good clones all along."

Although European growers have not forsaken famous place names in favor of that of the grape variety, they have consciously pursued greater varietalness of flavor in their traditional wines by choosing certain clones when replanting their vineyards. In Burgundy, Raymond Bernard, head of the Dijon Regional Center of the Office National Interprofessionnel des Vins de Table, has been in charge of an ambitious clonal selection project for Pinot Noir. He has identified over two hundred clones of Pinot Noir in the Burgundian vineyards. Of these, it was determined that only three or four clones were best. All of them gave good yields and their wines had pronounced varietal characteristics of raspberry, blackberry, and the like. Bernard believes that the best that can be done in clonal selection is eliminating undesirable clones from the mix.

Critics charge that part of the indefinable greatness of

Burgundian Pinot Noirs comes not only from distinctive soils, but from the ancient mix of having twenty or thirty different clones of Pinot Noir in the same small vineyard. Some of these clones, tasted alone, may not project much depth of flavor. Others have uneconomically low yields. But taken together, they add up to more than the sum of their parts. The thinking is that the subtle complications of Burgundy at its best, where the individual site shines through, has been overwhelmed by the blunt instrument of varietalness.

In Italy, which has perhaps the greatest number of grape varieties and clonal variations of any country, clonal differences and even whole varieties were almost willfully ignored. In Chianti, for example, vineyards were purchased by new landowners from Milan and Rome who were really looking for a country house, which in Chianti invariably come with a vineyard attached. They replanted the worn-out vineyard with whatever clone of Sangiovese the local nursery offered. Almost invariably, it was a lesser clone, frequently identified as Sangiovese Romagna, which is ostentatiously healthy and offers large yields of fat grapes. The wine, though, lacks depth and character. Long-established growers, greedy for high yields in a low-paying market, also planted the same clone, ignoring the lessons of the past.

When it was realized that the wines were inferior, many growers turned to Cabernet Sauvignon to achieve character, as well as follow fashion. Unlike Sangiovese, it has no real history in the area and is no better a grape than the best, small-berried clones of Sangiovese. But it does offer the quick fix of varietal flavor and deep color, as well as having the cachet of showing one's awareness of the trends of the outside world. Only in the late seventies did a reaction against the artificiality of Cabernet Sauvignon in Chianti set in. Even then, it took another decade before a serious clonal selection program for Sangiovese was established under university auspices. The hope is that when the vineyards again come due for replanting over the next fifteen or twenty years, the best strains of Sangiovese and other indigenous grapes such as Canaiolo and

Mammolo will have been identified and be broadly available on a commercial basis.

The other device used to create another version of varietalness, almost an instant identity kit, is the small (55-gallon/225-liter) new oak barrel, preferably made from oak grown in France. Because they flavor the wine with a pronounced vanilla taste and impart a round smoothness of style, the wine has an immediate familiarity about it, a reassuring sensation of déjà vu (or is it déjà *bu*?). The wine, regardless of grape variety or origin, is readily recognizable as being similar to—at least superficially—famous Bordeaux and Burgundies, where such small oak barrels are traditional. Many wines simply do not respond favorably to their use. The savor of site is jammed by the overriding signal of the barrel. The market appeal, however, is indisputable. Such wines have been franchised by the catniplike attraction of the small new oak barrels and the identifiable flavor and style they impart.

The problem is that an insistence on the franchised leads inevitably to the ersatz. I recall watching a television news feature about the rise of synthesizers in the music world. Apparently, computers have made great strides in synthesizing sounds. One person, working at the console of a synthesizer, can replicate an entire orchestra. Musicians playing the real thing, according to the newscast, are fast being thrown out of work.

To demonstrate the effectiveness of the synthesizer, a trumpet player was shown alongside a synthesizer operator, each performing the same trumpet solo. Viewers were commanded to discern the difference. The odd part was that a difference could be discerned, which doubtless was not the intent of the demonstration. The two sounds were close, uncannily so. But there *was* a difference and that difference was not a matter of rooting for the home team.

The underlying message was clear: Why bother to create something original and individual when you can just as easily copy it? This is not the same, it should be noted, as acknowledging that the world has always had lesser-quality reproductions of greater originals. In such instances there never was any doubt about the standing of the knock-off or the superiority and greater legitimacy of the original.

Now it is different. An increasing number of wines (and foods) are becoming so removed from the original inspiration that the ersatz has become the standard, while the original tastes odd and unappealing because of its unfamiliarity. This already has happened with bread, ham, beer, even fish. Today you can find so-called fish flakes constructed out of a paste that some people think are better than the real thing.

With music, one of the hot shows on television was—may still be—a competition called *Puttin' on the Hits*. Contestants are judged on the basis of their ability to look like, move like, and lip-sync the performance of a famous rock star. The ability to imitate is praised and rewarded as if it were as legitimate and desirable as the original performance. The wine version of *Puttin' on the Hits* is found in the numerous blind tastings where producers from an unheralded district take on the established stars of Burgundy or Bordeaux to prove that you can't tell their wines from the originals. What is being celebrated here? Not distinction, but the absence of it.

This comes from what might be called the mentality of varietalness. It affects how wines are judged and talked about. Varietalness is a great leveler. By focusing on it, the distinctions of site dissolve and become insignificant. No longer is it a matter of how singular a Meursault might be, but how good a Chardonnay it is. This, in turn, makes legitimate the notion that comparisons can be made without regard to source. The playing field has been leveled to where all wines are on the equal footing of variety.

Varietalness is the volume control of wine. The higher it's turned up, the more attention it attracts. In a wine judging—even of wines of the same type and origin—those wines in which the volume control is turned up, never mind what's playing, are most likely to be judged superior. Beethoven, from this perspective, always will triumph over Mozart.

An example of varietal mentality can be found in one wine newsletter's summary of the best red Burgundies from the 1985 vintage. The 1985 vintage in Burgundy was considered by all, including the newsletter writer, to be extraordinary. Lumping all the '85 red Burgundies together—they are all Pinot Noirs, after all—the writer listed 114 wines he considered the best of an extraordinary vintage. Closer examination revealed that just 18 wines, or 16 percent of the total, came from the Côte de Beaune. Everything else was from the Côte de Nuits.

Here we have a wine district, the Côte d'Or, which is composed of two subdistricts, the Côte de Nuits and the Côte de Beaune, each about fifteen miles long, which is the most fanatically site-specific wine-growing area in the world. Looking at this assessment, you would think that in 1985 the Côte de Beaune somehow didn't do as well as the Côte de Nuits. Yet this is not so. It did equally well, maybe even better than the Côte de Nuits. So how could it get such short shrift?

The answer is that collectively the Pinot Noirs of the Côte de Nuits are richer, more powerful wines than those of the Côte de Beaune. The fruit is bigger, more intense and, yes, the wines can be glorious. But in the mentality of varietalness, wines as sublime as Corton, Savigny-les-Beaune, Volnay, Beaune, Pommard, Chassagne-Montrachet, and Santenay—all from the Côte de Beaune—are bound to be also-rans. No matter how exquisite their composition, they never will have the varietal volume to take on the Wagnerian likes of Chambertin, Clos de la Roche, or Vosne-Romanée.

At issue here is not whether wines should be judged comparatively. They should. The issue is the nature and basis of the comparison. The mentality of varietalness dumps all of these lovingly distinguished Burgundies in the same cell, the tender Volnay "juvie" who ran his first stoplight with a hard-bitten recidivist Chambertin. It admits no distinction other than their both being Pinot Noirs of the same age from the same general neighborhood. A connoisseur's perspective would have summarized the best wines of the vintage by district, singling out the finest Beaunes in the legitimate context of Beaune, rather than other Pinot Noirs in the lineup—move along, please.

However gloomy the picture might appear—there is no sense pretending that all is blissful—the prospect for authentic, individual wines still is bright, perhaps brighter than it was twenty years ago when the threat was barely present. Its more obvious presence today has at least had a galvanizing effect. Also, it would be snobbery to assume that today's wine drinkers, in the long term, are any less desirous of what our ancestors wanted, what the painter Lucian Freud says he asks of a painting: "To astonish, disturb, seduce, convince." The only thing different now from prior generations is that today wine producers are able and—given the increasing competition—compelled to cater to the immediate needs and wants of the new audience. Science has given them that degree of control and the market has done the rest.

The demand will evolve. After all, one need only taste wines as disparate as Malvasia delle Lipari Passito from Carlo Hauner, with its haunting herbalness; a Château La Mission Haut-Brion of ripe age, which is an exquisite trumpet solo in the Bordeaux orchestra of great wines; a Chevalier-Montrachet, as refined and evolved as an alpine flower, from a producer as respectful as Louis Jadot or Georges Deleger; or something as seemingly humble as a Barbera from the Pianromualdo vineyard in the Barolo district, which in the hands of Vietti or Prunotto is luxurious enough to serve at a state dinner.

These and hundreds of other pleasures are not lost on today's wine drinkers. If anything, a movement is afoot to recapture or preserve some of the standards and glories of the past. At the same moment that Cabernet Sauvignon and Chardonnay threaten to overwhelm the vineyards of the world, a few producers in every vineyard area of note are more resolute than ever to ensure that the threat is no more than that.

These producers are not necessarily hidebound, nor are their wine-making methods always old-fashioned. The common denominator is that their efforts are toward a goal of greater expression of site than of ego, of diamondlike definition of flavor coupled with a depth that comes only from grapes grown to this end. Standing by them is an ever-larger number of wine lovers who seek out their wines; merchants who literally go the distance to find them; and, one hopes, enough writers who become sufficiently knowing about particular wines, districts, or regions to recognize these authentic voices when they hear them. This is happening.

It is happening in Burgundy, where a new generation of young winemakers, nearly all university-trained, have come to grips with the reality that Burgundies have degenerated and that big egos and even bigger prices do not make up for a squandered glory. They are bringing it back by replanting vineyards with ancient clonal variety; by vinifying their wines with artistry; by lowering their yields in exchange for concentration and depth in their wines. And they are being rewarded. Not only do they fetch more for their wines than lesser colleagues, but they have reaped a soul-satisfying recognition from an amazingly far-flung group of Burgundy lovers.

It is happening in Italy. Producers such as Piero Antinori, who initially championed the cause of Cabernet Sauvignon in Chianti, as well as many others who never lost faith, now are turning their backs on Cabernet in favor of pursuing their birthright Sangiovese. In Piedmont the fashion for small new oak barrels, new Chardonnay plantings, and fast fermentations to create easy-down-the-gullet, early-maturing Barolos and Barbarescos still is gaining. Yet the area remains anchored to its best traditions by enough producers whose wines are increasingly seen as the reference standards. Happily, these producers—Elvio Cogno of Marcarini; Bruno Giacosa, Aldo Conterno, Giacomo Conterno, Alfredo Currado of Vietti; Bartolo Mascarello, Giuseppe Colla of Prunotto, and many others—also command some of the highest prices, proof that a caring audience will support such effort.

It is happening in the Loire Valley and in Alsace, where chronic low prices have not deterred at least a few growers in every important village from pursuing the old standards. In the Loire this means producers such as Cotat in Chavignol; Joguet in Chinon; Lalanne and Baumard in Quarts de Chaume; Boivin in Bonnezeaux; Huet, Foreau and Poniatowski in Vouvray, among many others. In Alsace, the roll call includes such names as Trimbach, Zind-Humbrecht, Kientzler, Albrecht, Kreydenweiss, Ostertag, Bas, Mure, and many others.

The challenge is different in the New World. California and Pacific Northwest producers still are groping, simultaneously creating and following fashion. Certainly, the search for greater refinement in Cabernet and Chardonnay is under way in California. In Oregon the push for Pinot Noir is more intense than ever, with far finer wines than have yet been produced almost inevitable. Washington State seems to be producing ever-finer Semillon and Cabernet, two grape varieties for which it is not yet noted.

Australia, too, is evolving from the blood-and-guts wines of old into something more polished and restrained. Caught at the moment in the Cabernet and Chardonnay whirl, Australian wine producers nevertheless are proceeding in a fashion different from that of California. Where California at the moment is investigating the subtle effects of specialized vinification and barrel-aging techniques, Australia seems more convinced than ever that its path lies in preserving essential fruit flavors and aromas. For both Australia and California it is too soon to say where these paths will lead, except that the trend in both cases is away from the excess of the earlier wines.

It is impossible not to believe that an increasing number

of wine drinkers will seek what wine lovers have always found most rewarding: wines of austerity in youth that achieve fullness and depth with age. The steady diet of Cabernet and Chardonnay will give way to a search for different or at least finer sensations. Security, like crutches, will be flung aside in search of delight, astonishment, seduction, the delicious disturbance of variety. It won't happen all at once—it can't— but such is the provocativeness of fine wine that it is inevitable.

3. Appellation and Authenticity

A world of made is not a world of born.

—e. e. cummings
"1 × 1 (One Times One)"

One of the truths of wine is appellation. Like all truths, it is not so much absolute as enduring. Ideally, appellations identify areas sharing attributes that result in a commonality of taste. These include factors such as sunshine, rainfall, soil type and structure, exposure, and elevation, among other variables. In this scheme, it is the location of the vineyard, along with the selection of the grape varieties best suited for it, that matters most. The winemaker here is more servant than master.

The most exquisitely detailed appellations, like those of the Côte d'Or in Burgundy or Germany's Mosel/Saar/Ruwer, may be likened to the frequencies of a radio band. When isolated and "tuned in" with the right grape varieties, we can receive even the breathiest whispers of the Earth in a way not possible by any other means. Appellations are the mapping of the source and strength of the signal.

That the establishment of appellations is now under way in every wine-growing state in America—about forty—as well as in Australia, New Zealand, indeed just about everywhere in the New World, underscores the importance of appellation. Without it, wines exist in a gravity-free state, without the pull of place that allows us to trace and track the possible reasons for its distinction.

To do this right, however, takes an inhumanly long time. Compared to the leisurely pace of wine and vines, we are a fleeting presence. By the time a vineyard is planted and begins to bear fruit (four years); by the time the vine reaches true maturity and its roots are deep (fifteen years); by the time an age-worthy wine of quality achieves its most vocal expression (anywhere from five to twenty-five years)— well, we witnesses are almost out of time. As winemakers so often lament, how many vintages are there in the life of a winemaker? Thirty? Forty? And of these, how many will he or she see through from harvest to full-fledged maturity? Maybe half.

As a result, appellation is also a form of immortality. It is a collection of insights handed down through multiple generations and subject to vetting by the latest one. This almost Confucian interaction between past and present evolves into a consensus about place and grape that becomes the cartography of taste called appellation.

The problem today is that new or uncharted wine-growing areas do not have the luxury of this collective, finely sifted memory. Commercial pressures, as well as the hurriedness of the age, make establishing appellations a quick, makeshift job. If the name Napa Valley translates to a higher price—which it does—then who is entitled to use that name becomes a pressing matter. Lines must be drawn, if only to protect one's investment or, further down the road, profit from it when the time comes to sell a vineyard or expand a label. Whether there is a commonality of taste is beside the point; it's a matter of fence-building. Right now, the map superimposed on virtually all new wine-growing areas reflects politics and economics rather than commonality of taste. Future cartographers of taste presumably will realign things using the longitude and latitude of wine itself.

But why the title "Appellation and Authenticity"? Simply because the one helps deliver the other. Because of appellation, we now enjoy the most authentic wines yet created. This is to say that the odds are better today than ever in the history of commercial wine making that what's in the bottle actually comes from the place declared on the label.

The importance of authenticity cannot be overestimated. Without it, wine is just another anonymous beverage, like orange juice. Precisely because grapevines, unlike orange trees, are so sensitive to their site, our appreciation is inextricably tied to source. Because appellations are a consensus involving both site and grape, it is not enough merely to point to a spot, like an overseer to a gold prospector, saying, "Dig here." To have meaning and worth, appellations have to deliver the goods. This means being involved with which grapes can be grown on the site, how they are raised and, later, handled through to bottling. As a result, the phrase seen today in France, Italy, and Spain, among other very old wine-growing nations, is not just appellation of origin, but *controlled* appellation of origin: *appellation d'origine controlée* (France) or *denominazione d'origine controllata* (Italy), among others.

In the United States the federally mandated phrase—under the aegis of the Bureau of Alcohol, Tobacco and Firearms—is American Viticultural Area or AVA, which is revealingly devoid of the term *controlled*. This is because there aren't any controls. Appellations in the United States, as well as in Australia and New Zealand, are in the embryonic stage of simple line-drawing. No controls exist forbidding or requiring certain grape varieties in particular sites, nor for yields, pruning methods, or vinification techniques. It is too soon, to say nothing of antagonistic to the culture.

You would think that legally defined appellations of origin are almost as old as wine itself. Instead, the first instance of controlled appellations of origin did not appear until 1911, in France. And this pioneering effort only spread to equally old wine-growing countries such as Italy and Spain in the 1960s and 1970s, respectively.

The reason that legal appellations appeared so astonishingly late is that the demand for fine wine, which is to say wine from a pinpointed source, was not until recently so great as to unduly distort the honesty of producers, shippers, and merchants. Fraudulent wines are inevitable and have appeared throughout history. The question here is one of degree. The push for appellations came to shove and eventually to riot when the degree of fraud reached epidemic proportions in the early 1900s. But the cause of the epidemic of fraud first appeared in 1863.

What happened then was the introduction into France of the sap-sucking root louse called *Phylloxera vastatrix*. It came from the United States in a shipment of grapevine cuttings originally sent to England in 1863. Within thirty years, phylloxera had decimated the entire European winefield. This was achieved by the near-microscopic bug sucking the life out of the European grapevines, all of which are from the *Vitis vinifera* family. Their roots had no inborn resistance to the foreign bug, unlike the thirty-five varieties of native American grapes such as *Vitis rupestris* or *Vitis labrusca*.

In the Europe of the 1870s, 1880s, and 1890s the vineyards slowly withered. It happened sequentially and catastrophically, the root louse making its way fitfully from region to region. Every unaffected area thought it was exempt—until it learned otherwise. When the growers finally did see its appearance in their own vineyards—the grapevines simply dried up—they could do nothing about it. They tried, of course. They used all sorts of chemical treatments:

sprays, injections, flooding, fumigations. Nothing worked. After immense worry and uncountable financial loss, European winegrowers came to the solution of last resort: grafting their *vinifera* varieties onto American rootstocks. To this day, it still is the only effective means of thwarting phylloxera. The cost to the winegrower was barely, if at all, supportable: up to two thousand French francs an acre at the time. This was when, in 1899, a laborer made just sixty francs a month and even the greatest wines, such as Clos de Vougeot, sold for six hundred francs a barrel, according to Agoston Haraszthy writing in 1862. With a few isolated exceptions, particularly in Germany where certain soils are unreceptive to the phylloxera bug, virtually every vine planted in Europe has first been painstakingly grafted onto an American rootstock. The process will continue until someone comes up with a different, equally effective means of combating phylloxera.

The wine production of the most famous vineyards and districts in France declined, as it did elsewhere. The numbers, dry as they are, reveal the extent of the undoing: From 1870 to 1900 the vineyard area of France declined by 64 percent. In a similar period, its yields decreased 61 percent, from an average yield of 24.5 hectoliters per hectare to just 15.2 hectoliters per hectare.

But the public thirst for wine did not decline. In fact, it grew steadily. Wine consumption in France more than doubled, from 51 liters per capita in 1848 to 103 liters in 1904. The result was massive fraud. Wines labeled as coming from Burgundy or Bordeaux came instead from Algeria, Italy, or Spain, if they were wine at all. They might instead have been concoctions spawned in a warehouse somewhere. According to Theodore Zeldin in *France 1848–1945*, Volume II, "When in 1880 the municipal laboratories of Paris tested 300 samples of wine bought at random in local bars, they found 225 of them to be seriously adulterated, 50 slightly so, and only 25 to be pure."

The degree and extent of fraud grew so bad by the late 1800s that there emerged an anger so intense from the many grape growers of France that it nearly brought down the government. The flash point was in Champagne. Although phylloxera came late to the Champagne vineyards—only in 1890—it loomed as a threat and its effects elsewhere magnified the sense of urgency. But it was fraud, rather than phylloxera, that caused the outburst: a flagrant flouting of the then-unwritten covenant between grape growers and winemakers that the name on the label should reflect the wines of the place.

This did not happen in the Champagne region, where the big Champagne houses were enjoying an unprecedented boom in sales. Instead, they purchased cheaper grapes from outside the region to augment their more expensive supplies from within it. It was fraud on a huge and organized scale, so much so that it is estimated that the Champagne houses were annually selling twelve million more bottles of wine labeled as coming from Champagne than the district could possibly have produced. It went on for years.

Finally, in 1911, the winegrowers of Champagne could take no more. Their anger was detonated by a Senate action that rescinded—at the urging of the powerful Champagne houses—an earlier, feeble effort to establish legal boundaries of appellation. Frustrated at this betrayal, the growers rampaged through the streets of Aÿ, a small but important wine town in the heart of Champagne, looting and destroying the stocks of every Champagne house suspected—rightly or wrongly—of purchasing wine from outside the traditional borders of Champagne.

France was shocked by the riot, which riveted the nation's attention to the general grievances of its winegrowers everywhere. The attention was so intense and demanding that only eight weeks after the riot the government established a legal definition of the boundaries of Champagne. Even more important, it confirmed that the valuable name of Champagne on a wine bottle belonged exclusively to the district defined and no other. With this, the first legal blow was struck in the name of authenticity.

No sooner was this accomplished than the First World

War arrived and after it, the disrupted French economy of the 1920s. But French winegrowers did not forget the small advances made since the riots of 1911. Various laws and amendments were passed in the intervening years, but they were merely palliative. The growers wanted a cure for the infection of fraud. Despite everything, it reemerged after the war even more viciously than it had before it, especially during the late twenties and the Depression years of the thirties. Once again, wines bearing the names of famous appellations—which by then existed under the law but in the loosest fashion—bore no resemblance to the genuine article. And growers of the genuine article looked on in dismay and, increasingly, poverty.

The first blow for real change was struck in Châteauneuf-du-Pape in 1923, under the visionary leadership of Baron LeRoy of Château Fortia. Long victims of fraud because of its widely recognized name, the producers of Châteauneuf-du-Pape undertook on their own the definition of their own boundaries and, more important yet, legal prescriptions of which grape varieties could be used for a wine selling under the name of Châteauneuf-du-Pape, how these vines were to be pruned and trained, the minimum ripeness required of grapes at harvest time, and various other key ingredients to authenticity and quality. It served as a model for the national system that was to appear thirteen years later.

In the meantime, growers to the north of Châteauneuf-du-Pape, in the fabled Côte d'Or of Burgundy, were battling the shippers of the area, who had had a stranglehold on the commerce of Burgundy since the Revolution. The *négociants*, or shippers, had long purchased young wines from the numerous small growers of the area and blended various lots of wines to sell under their own label. Ideally, only different lots of, say, Volnay, should be sold under that name. But in practice, the shippers blended what they liked in order to create a wine that corresponded to what the public considered a Volnay. Just how the public came to its conclusion about what Volnay should taste like reveals the chicken-and-egg aspect of the situation, as the only source of the wine was the shippers.

If this blending had been limited only to Pinot Noir wines from the Côte d'Or, probably everything would have continued as before. Instead, the shippers pursued more ardently than ever their historical practice of baptizing the light, delicate Pinot Noir wines with the stronger, deeper-colored red wines of the nearby Rhône Valley, made from such grapes as Syrah and Grenache. Also, the Rhône wines were far cheaper. These blends then were sold under the most famous Burgundian place names, such as Volnay, Chambertin, Pommard, and the like.

A few growers protested publicly, such as the Marquis d'Angerville in Volnay, Henri Gouges in Nuits St.-Georges, Jacques Matrot in Meursault, and Armand Rousseau in Gevrey-Chambertin, who formed a growers' organization, the Union Générale des Syndicats pour la Défense des Producteurs de Grands Vins de Bourgogne, which took some of the shippers to court. They were cut dead by the *négociants*, who blackballed such troublemakers, refusing to buy their wines. The courage of these and a few other growers is the more apparent when one recalls that their stand was made in the late 1920s and the 1930s, when the Depression stifled sales to the extent that no less a wine than Chambertin had to be made into a sparkling wine in order to sell. Since the shippers had more wine in their cellars than they had clients, refusing to buy the latest vintage from obstreperous growers handily dovetailed with their own needs.

Finally, in 1935 a law was passed establishing the Institut National des Appellations d'Origine des Vins et Eaux-de-Vie, now invariably referred to as INAO, under the Ministry of Agriculture. Its charge was to establish, based upon formal petitions from representative groups of growers, legally defined appellation boundaries, along with a codification of grape-growing and wine-making practices appropriate to the area. These boundaries and practices were established, with no little wrangling, as might be imagined, under the umbrella philosophy of *loyal, locale et constant*—traditional, individual to the area, and demonstrably long-term. It was a monumental task, entailing not just endless adjudication of conflicting interests—grower, shipper, and consumer—but massive technical demands. Some twelve thousand maps had to be drawn, charting the nooks and crannies of each appellation of origin, which currently number about 380.

Naturally, one of its tasks was the elimination of fraud—now finally defined with clarity—which is the responsibility of the enforcement arm of INAO, called the Service de la Répression des Fraudes et du Contrôle de la Qualité. It, like INAO itself, is funded by a tax on all wines produced in France and is therefore self-supporting. Although its efforts, inevitably, are less than perfect, the fact remains that fraudulent wines are far more difficult to pass off today than before.

Today, the discipline exercised by various appellation authorities, in France as well as in Italy, Germany, and Spain, is widely considered to be excessive. Growers in these and other countries cannot deviate in the slightest degree from the Talmudic prescriptions of how they should carry out their professional lives. Only certain grapes may be grown; pruned only in a certain authorized fashion; vinified and treated in prescribed manners, and so forth. Many of these regulations are admirable, but no sooner do you seek to close one loophole than another emerges, necessitating yet another regulation. The legalities of European wine growing are boggling in number and complexity.

Making matters even more complicated is the effort to unify various national wine regulations into a pan-European collection of wine laws among nations in the European Economic Community (EEC) or Common Market. This has not been at all easy, what with Germany's needs being very different from those of, say, Italy. The French tend to hold sway, much to the chafing dismay of other member groups. But the process now is largely complete and no member nation can enact wine laws that contradict those of the EEC.

This long march toward authenticity through controlled appellations has given way to an ironic luxury: an urge toward anarchy. All anarchists need a government, and the controlled appellation movement has obliged in spades. Since no one now questions the authenticity of wine, the only thing left is to question whether what is required represents the best the land can offer. Here the modern demand for self-expression clashes with the profound conservatism of controlled appellations. After all, the whole idea of controlled appellations was to protect what was once under siege.

So now, numerous wine critics contend that the *who* of wine making is more important than the *where* of wine growing. Since the where is now plausibly ensured, it is a seductive argument. Just as prosperity and relative peace allowed the Renaissance to flourish, giving rise to a notion of man as the focus of life, so too has the peace and prosperity of controlled appellations allowed this secular view of wine to emerge, a conviction of man as not just triumphant, but seminal. The most graphic example of this, literally, is the label for the new Napa Valley wine called Dominus. Created by Christian Moueix, whose family owns Château Pétrus, the label for Dominus, a Cabernet-based red wine, is dominated by a full-length drawing of Moueix over which is imposed his signature. The message is unmistakable.

The vehicle for this expression of the who is the other great wine revolution of the twentieth century: *domaine* or estate bottling. *Domaine* bottling and controlled appellations enjoy a symbiotic relationship. One without the other is an empty accomplishment. Estate-bottled wines give meaning to appellation boundaries in that the appearance of different bottlings all retaining a familial similarity demonstrates the insight of appellation. For its part, controlled appellation provides a meaningful calling card, namely the appellation itself. Also there is the critical protection against fraud, without which the producer creating the authentic article is helpless and at an economic and aesthetic disadvantage. Of course, human incompetence can render even the most acute appellation insight worthless. This happens too often—Burgundy is a choice example—but the blame is easily fixed. Appellations are to wine what an editor is to a writer: You cannot blame the editor for a writer's lack of ability. Appellations, like editors, can offer focus, no more.

Prior to estate bottling, virtually all commercial wines came from shippers who bought grapes or wines, then blended and sold them under their own label. In the case of the famous properties of Bordeaux, they used the name of the château, but it was the shipper who performed all of the cellaring and bottling tasks that are so critical to the eventual quality and taste of the wine.

That the growers nurtured a dislike, even a hatred, of the all-powerful shippers—no matter what the region—is easily understood. Less evident, though, is the degree to which these shippers defined our vision of certain wines—sometimes for the better, sometimes not. Because virtually all wines passed through their hands and because their interests were more mercantile than devoted to the land, we received wines suited to a broad taste. This is not to suggest that a few shippers did not, in fact, offer authentic wines, but rather, that the majority of the offerings of even the most famous names were happily manipulated to suit the desires of the target market.

In this respect the shippers were completely honest. Champagne houses noted on their labels that especially dry or Brut bottlings were made "Special for the English Market." Burgundy shippers were notorious for acceding to the English demand for "worked-on" wines, a practice that flourished openly, if illegally, right up to the entry of Great Britain into the Common Market in 1973. After that, the practice declined because Common Market controls made it more difficult to ship such wines safely to Britain. Nor is this accommodation to individual markets a recent development. In the nineteenth century a wine as fine as Château

Lafite was augmented with a dose of red Hermitage. For this the client paid extra and the wine was referred to as being *hermitagé*. Cyrus Redding, in *Every Man His Own Butler* (1852), felt free to reveal that "the Bordeaux wines sent to England are not pure growths, but mixed with second-class hermitage, and sometimes beni-carlo, adding a little spirit of wine [brandy]." Benicarló is a Spanish village on the Mediterranean once noted for its deeply colored, heavy red wines which, as Redding pointed out, were popular for blending with lighter-hued Bordeaux.

Whether growers liked any of this was moot: They had no choice. Only the shippers had the resources, enough wine even, to reach out to markets beyond the area of production. Only the shippers had access to the upper-class clientele who were the audience for the best wines. The social savvy, language skills, and the capital to own large stocks of wines was far beyond the horizons of even the most ambitious grower.

Added to this was the technical matter of seeing the wine-making process through to its final moment of bottling. The majority of growers had no idea of how to go about it. Cellaring and bottling wines were unpracticed arts to them, especially on a commercial scale. What growers made for themselves was likely a far cry in terms of cleanliness and quality from what sophisticated foreign markets demanded.

In Alsace, for example, growers to this day deliver only grapes to the many shippers of the region. In Burgundy, the growers do vinify (make) the wine, but then sell off the barrels only weeks after the primary fermentation is completed. This is why the famous Hospice de Beaune auction is held so early after the harvest, on the third Saturday in November.

In Bordeaux, the estates made the wine according to the instructions provided by the shippers, who even published simple little texts for them with titles like *Faire du Bon Vin* (How to Make Good Wine) to teach the growers the basics of sound wine making. Afterward, the barrels would be delivered to the shipper's warehouse in the city of Bordeaux to be *élevé*, or raised, as the French refer to the practice of cellaring, hence the frequently seen term *négociant-éleveur*. The same word, *élever*, also is applied to the raising and education of French children.

Not to be forgotten is the capital tie-up involved. In the nineteenth century red wines typically were left in wood casks or barrels for as long as five or six years. Even today, the best red wines spend between eighteen to twenty-four months in wood. This is in addition to any cellaring in bottle, as is still required for wines such as Barolo and Brunello di Montalcino, where a three- or four-year aging period before release is mandatory. A grower living from the proceeds of one crop to the next who has already spent money on sprays, fertilizer, new vines, labor, barrels, and so forth is hardly in a position to tie up his capital for several years, even if he could eventually sell it himself.

The revolution that is *domaine* bottling first began in the late 1920s. In Bordeaux it started with the singular effort of the late Baron Philippe de Rothschild who, in 1926, somehow convinced the owners of Châteaux Lafite, Haut-Brion, Margaux, Latour, and Yquem to no longer send their unfinished wines to the shippers, but instead bottle it themselves. He must have been marvelously persuasive, considering that he was very much an outsider, ridiculously young (twenty-four years old), and Mouton was then not even a First Growth (it achieved this unprecedented upgrade in 1973). But for Rothschild, his wine was to be a personal expression, and that was impossible as long as somebody else was cellaring and bottling it. Lesser Bordeaux estates did not estate-bottle until the 1960s, for reasons that will soon be apparent.

The same pattern can be found throughout France and Italy, with the vast majority of estates releasing their own wines under their own labels only very recently. In fact, their number still is increasing substantially in these countries, with estate bottling yet to take hold in Spain and Portugal. When it does, as is inevitable, the effects will be explosive.

Although the installment of appellations was critical for the success of estate-bottled wines, it was not the empowering agent. That was economics. Wine prices had to rise in order for growers to be able to afford to make, cellar, and bottle their production. And customers had to come to them. With the European economic boom of the 1960s, these two ingredients coalesced. Middle-class Europeans of newfound wealth began to travel for the first time, aided by the opening of freeways. For Burgundian growers it was a bonanza, as the autoroute to the South of France meant that Danes, Dutch, Belgians, Germans, French, and Swiss drove right through Burgundy. For growers it was the equivalent of salmon wriggling through a narrow channel. To net them, all they needed to do was hang out a sign: *vente directe*—direct sale.

Other districts also had their tourism, such as the Loire. In Italy, the economic boom meant greater travel by Italians within the country and an increased appreciation for its best wines. Those districts without tourism—Bordeaux, for example—found a new audience through mail order. Wine clubs emerged, offering members deals on previously unknown wines or producers, which provided yet another outlet.

Not to be dismissed was the immense effect of the entry of America into the European market. Although wine consumption in the United States in the 1960s and early 1970s was minimal compared to that of Europe, the American audience was well off, wanted only the best wines, and was prepared to pay. Increasingly, major corporations with their own substantial capital sought to bypass the shippers. Since the shipper's edge was always a matter of capital reserves and big American corporations had their own, thank you, they simply went straight to the source. This had a revolutionary effect in Bordeaux and changed forever the manner in which the wines of the area were sold to foreign clients. By the late seventies, the once-omnipotent shippers had been reduced to the role of go-betweens, carrying out the minor paperwork details on behalf of the new regime.

In Burgundy, reluctant growers were urged by a handful of American importers to bottle at least part of their production—preferably the best-quality part—under their own label. Importers such as the late Frank Schoonmaker and, later on, Alexis Lichine (who has since sold the company bearing his name), were significant figures in increasing the number of *domaine*-bottled Burgundies. America, more than any other country, has been the longest-standing market for these wines.

The economic prosperity of the sixties, seventies, and eighties in the Western world has resulted in a massive revision of the way we think about wine, where it is made, and how it is made. California wine growing exploded in the seventies when wealthy outsiders to wine became entranced with its possibilities, both aesthetic and commercial, and sluiced enormous sums into vineyards and brand-new wineries. The result is now well known. Similar, if less lavish, efforts proceeded in other states, most notably in Oregon, Washington, and New York.

In Europe, no country has transformed its wines more completely than Italy, where a similar infusion of outside wealth and new ideas overturned the musty traditionalism of the past. Italian consumers, many of whom are newly wealthy, are prepared to pay prices once considered impossible for Italian wines. Foreign clients, especially Germans, Swiss, and Americans, are no less willing.

Because so many of these new efforts everywhere in the world, from Australia to California to Italy, operate without preconceived notions of what is traditional or even commercial, the resulting wines have challenged the Establishment. In some cases the new wines are merely flashy. But a significant number prove the worth of the effort. Chiantis, for example, are emerging like a newly restored old painting once covered with grime. The grime was the oxidized dreariness of the old style: The restoration has come with the challenge of the new order, which pursues vibrant, 100 percent-Sangiovese wines as opposed to the old-style blend of Sangiovese and the white-wine grape Trebbiano. In America, Pinot Noirs from Oregon have revised the standard by which Californians must judge their efforts. California Chardonnays, in turn, have jolted the French from their self-satisfied complacency. And within each locale, new arrivals set a new standard—even in such places as Burgundy and Bordeaux, where a new generation throws over the earlier parental methods and exposes a previously unsuspected potential from ancient vineyard holdings.

Although it is apparent that shippers have contributed mightily to much of the malfeasance of the past, it would be wrong to conclude today that shippers are either incapable of competing with the best domains or estates or that they have continued their past practices. One of the important side effects of estate bottling has been a competition shippers had never known before. Many of them have risen to the challenge, creating genuinely authentic wines that compete with the best bottlings from any source. Burgundy *négociants* such as Leroy, Jadot, Drouhin, Faiveley, and Labouré-Roi have redoubled their efforts and their wines are better than ever. In the Rhône, you can do no better than the shipper Guigal; in Italy the family company of Masi, outside Verona, creates wines that are standard-bearers in the region; Bruno Giacosa and Prunotto do the same in the Piedmont. The list continues everywhere in the world: Robert Mondavi in California; Lindeman's in Australia; Cordier in Bordeaux. But the benchmark for authenticity now is the *domaine*-bottled wine, a development these shippers' grandparents would never have dreamed possible.

Viewed from the despairing perspective of a wine lover witnessing the disaster of phylloxera, World War I, Prohibition in the United States, the Depression, and then World

War II—a span of seventy years between 1880 and 1950—the vitality of wine today seems almost an impossibility. Yet it is fair to suggest that this is a Golden Age of wine. Never before have wine lovers been able to get as close to the source. And never before have as many sources been revealed or made available as exist today. The pursuit of authenticity in wine has never been a happier chase.

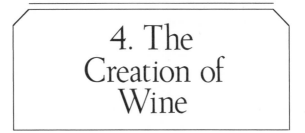

4. The Creation of Wine

Whatever happens, the earth will continue to renew itself and mankind will find reasons for living in the constants that survive wars, government, revolution and all historic changes. Everywhere, the things that last are more astonishing than the things that pass.

—Anne O'Hare McCormick

Nothing about wine is more lasting—or astonishing—than fermentation. The process is simple: Yeasts, which are single-celled plants, consume the sugar in grape juice and transform it into roughly equal parts of alcohol and carbon dioxide gas. If the gas is liberated, as it is in an open vat, we get still wine. If the gas is trapped, we get sparkling wine.

The usual treatises on how wine is made focus on just that: the technology of how it is *made*. This is misleading. As Roger Boulton of the University of California at Davis Department of Viticulture and Enology puts it, "Ninety percent of winemaking has nothing to do with the winemaker. All a winemaker is doing is preventing spoilage, introducing some style characteristics and bottling it." All of the shiny equipment one sees in a modern winery—stainless steel tanks, centrifuges, gleaming oak barrels, sterile bottling lines with nitrogen-purging capability—are designed to prevent spoilage, add a lagniappe of style, and put the wine in bottles.

These efforts are essential and are part of the craft of wine making. But to really understand how wine gets made, as opposed to preserved, you need only understand fermentation. Everything else is flourish. This is why this chapter on the creation of wine is so titled. How does wine get created? What are the life forces—for that is what they are—that transubstantiate grapes into wine? For these are the things that last, that are more astonishing than the technologies that pass.

Yeasts are central to wine in a way that nothing else, short of grapes, can claim. Wine making is a dance with yeasts. The winemaker partners it by moving it into a vessel where it comes into contact with grape juice; by coaxing it to move faster or slower by means of temperature control; keeps its attentions from flagging by giving it air or feeding it sugar and nutrients such as vitamins and minerals.

Even after the fermentation is complete, the waltz continues, as the winemaker seeks first to extract any additional flavor from the dead yeast cells through the process of autolysis, in which the cells decompose and excrete their constituents into the wine. Or by the elimination of these cells by racking. Or by the use of yet another fermentation, this time in a tightly sealed bottle or tank, to create a sparkling wine. Much of cellaring practice is a process of getting yeasts on and off the dance floor of wine as gracefully as possible. And then keeping them off to prevent unwanted refermentation or spoilage.

The phenomenon of fermentation must surely have been one of the longest-standing mysteries of civilization. We live, and have always lived, in a world swirling with airborne wild yeasts and bacteria. It is believed that the flavor enhancement of fermentation affected prehistoric wheat porridges. Centuries later, the Egyptians recognized the leavening effect fermentation could have on bread. By 2600 B.C., sourdough-bread–making was a methodical, if misunderstood, practice. As the English physicist John Tyndall remarked in 1876 on the ancient mystery of fermentation, "Our prehistoric fathers may have been savages, but they were clever and observant ones."

This is more generous than some of the current crop of self-congratulatory scientists. The most that Professor Emile Peynaud, formerly of the University of Bordeaux, who is the most influential enologist or wine scientist in France, will grudge is that before the discoveries of Louis Pasteur in the mid-1800s, "Good wine was merely the result of a succession of lucky accidents." Since virtually every great wine of France today, to say nothing of Italy and Germany, was already being made by then, we can only conclude from this that our ancestors were improbably lucky.

Fermentation remained a trial-and-error mystery for millennia until 1857, when Louis Pasteur first read his paper called "Memoir on Lactic Fermentation" to the Scientific Society of Lille. It was published the following year. In it he initiated the overthrow of the conventional wisdom that held that spontaneous generation was the cause of fermentation, rather than a life force. But we are getting ahead of our story.

The beginning of the tale could be said to have started in 1680 when the Dutch naturalist and inventor of the microscope, Anton van Leeuwenhoek, turned his microscopic attentions to yeast cells. What he discovered was that globules of some kind of microscopic life existed. There matters remained until superior microscopes were invented and used by inquiring minds. This took another century and a half when, in 1835, Charles Cagniard de la Tour in France and, independently, Schwann in Germany, discovered these yeast cells to be multiplying by budding before their eyes. They were looking at deposits left in beer vats. The question immediately raised was: Does fermentation have anything to do with these obviously alive microorganisms? Cagniard de la Tour concluded that fermentation was the result of yeast growth and therefore a living process rather than a lifeless chemical one.

Yet the inquiry was dropped. The problem was that such a notion was contrary to all of the many theories of the day. Fifty years before, the great French chemist Antoine Laurent Lavoisier postulated that alcoholic fermentation was a chemical matter. He observed that, between the carbon dioxide gas produced and the amount of alcohol created, all of the fermentable sugar was accounted for. From this he concluded that fermentation was caused by a chemical splitting of the sugar molecule. This notion of a chemical cause, rather than a life force, was the popular and widely held notion. It was itself part of a larger belief in spontaneous generation, which seemed to so many to be self-evident.

So in 1857, when Louis Pasteur was just thirty-four years old, he was taking on the scientific heavies of his day and their predecessors. Only shortly before Pasteur entered the fray, the eminent Swedish chemist Jöns Berzelius coined the word *catalyst* from the Greek *katalysis*, or dissolution. The idea of a catalyst, good to this day, is that of a substance that accelerates a change of another substance without itself being changed. With this idea, Berzelius then held that yeasts—which he recognized as living organisms—actually were catalysts. By their mere presence in a sugary liquid, according to Berzelius, they broke down the sugar into alcohol and carbon dioxide, but not by any biological action on their part. Yeasts, in other words, were innocent, if catalytic, bystanders in the lifeless process of fermentation.

As if Berzelius, who died in 1848, was not luminary enough, Justus von Leibig, a German chemist who was the towering figure in his field, supported the Berzelius supposition with a twist of his own: the force of decay. He insisted that the yeasts acted as catalysts, but through the process of putrefaction. According to von Leibig, the yeasts died and their rotting caused fermentation. "It is the dead portion of the yeast, which has been alive and is in process of alteration, that acts on the sugar," said von Liebig. Unfortunately for Pasteur, von Leibig lived until 1873 and clutched his theory to the end. By then Pasteur had long since proved it wrong, but von Leibig's prestigious and aggressive opposition didn't help matters any.

The stature of von Leibig was such that it was not co-incidence that Pasteur's assault on the theories of a chemical or putrefactive cause for fermentation occurred not with beer or wine, but with sour milk. In impugning supporters of the "vitalistic" or biological school of fermentation, von Leibig noted the absence of any yeasts when milk soured. At the time no distinction was drawn between souring and ferment-ing. Through careful microscopic studies Pasteur found tiny cells reproducing in soured milk. He considered these to be lactic acid yeasts. In fact they are bacteria. But the important thing was that they were alive. And Pasteur was able to dem-onstrate that their inclusion in unsoured milk rapidly led to souring, a vitalistic cause.

Then he turned his microscopic sights to alcoholic fer-mentation and, in a feat of imaginative laboratory demonstra-tion, showed how yeasts would grow and reproduce—and cause a fermentation—on a medium that could not putrefy. This was presented to the world in 1859 in Pasteur's landmark *Note on Alcoholic Fermentation*. Von Leibig refused to accept the evidence.

With a life force now proved to be the cause of fermen-tation and spontaneous generation a myth, Pasteur discovered something about yeasts that was boggling: They can live with-out oxygen. This led him to offer his now-famous declaration that "fermentation is life without oxygen." This is not quite the case, since yeasts perform better in the presence of oxygen than in its absence, but Pasteur was the first to recognize that fermentation could be *aerobic* (with oxygen) or *anaerobic* (with-out oxygen). In fact, yeasts do not need oxygen for fermen-tation; they need it only for reproduction.

What Pasteur did not know, and did not live long enough to see discovered, was that yeasts, per se, do not cause fer-mentation. Berzelius was not entirely off track with his notion about catalysts, although he had no idea of what form it even-tually would take. Neither did two German brothers, Eduard and Hans Buchner, both chemists, who in 1897 during a search for an extract for a medicine took yeast cells and put them through a grinding medium of sand and a type of silicon-rich earth called kieselguhr.

After they ground up the yeast cells they squeezed out the "extract" in a hydraulic press. The problem was preserving the extract. In a nice, homey touch they chanced on using sugar, recalling how well preserved high-sugar solutions such as jams can be, for reasons that will be explained shortly. So the juicy extract was mixed with sugar. The result was a bafflement worthy of Sherlock Holmes: "When you have eliminated the impossible, whatever remains, however improbable, must be the truth." What remained was improbable yet true: The sugar had fermented. Alcohol and carbon dioxide were forming—without life. Ten years later, after a great deal more laboratory work, Eduard Buchner was awarded a Nobel prize for his discovery of "cell-less fermentation."

What the Buchner brothers had discovered already had a name, given to it in 1878 by another German of remarkable insight, Wilhelm Kühne. Although he had not devised a means of isolating it from yeast, and thereby proving its existence as the Buchners did, Kuhne did recognize that there was a catalyst at work in the yeasts that caused the fermentation. This catalyst he called an enzyme, coining the word from the Greek *en* (in) and *zume* (yeast). The discovery of enzymes improbably brought the two mutually antagonistic theories of lifeless fermentation and vitalism together, in an odd sort of way.

It is enzymes secreted by the yeasts that create fermentation. You can ferment a wine without it ever seeing a yeast cell, should you care to take the trouble. It is, however, far easier to introduce enzymes into grape juice through the originating vehicle of yeasts than any other possible method. The role of enzymes is the key to fermentation. As catalysts, substances that accelerate a chemical reaction without themselves being changed, it is enzymes that transform grape juice into wine.

The actual process is complicated, involving at least thirty different chemical reactions, a dominolike process in which each reaction is dependent upon a preceding one. Each reaction is the work of one enzyme only, each of which is so specialized that it affects one substance and that one only. For example, the enzyme called protease works only on protein; invertase breaks down sucrose; and for wine, the most important of all is zymase, which is a single name applied to a large number of enzymes. Zymase, in all of its constituent enzymes, is considered the source of fermentation whereby sugar is converted into alcohol. The name zymase, coined by Buchner, has since been redefined to refer to just one enzyme among the many involved in fermentation, but the term still has resonance because of Buchner's discovery.

Astonishing though this discovery was—and still is—one thing about wine is always consistent: Yeasts remain the source of all that a winemaker needs to transform grape juice into wine. They are an unlikely vehicle, superficially one of the simplest forms of life. A typical wine yeast is about 8 microns by 7 microns, a measurement—if this means anything—equaling 8/25,000ths of an inch by 7/25,000ths of an inch. To see one under a microscope, at least with any definition, a magnification of 400 to 900 diameters is needed. Their quantity in fermenting grape juice is so fantastic as to beggar the imagination: One drop can contain five million yeasts. And when conditions are right, they can double their number in two hours.

Yeasts make wine inevitable. In all of the ancient vineyard areas of the world, wine making proceeds, even in the presence of the most advanced equipment, as it did when the first wines were made. In Burgundy, which has been making wines for millennia, the *vigneron* harvests his grapes, crushes them to rupture the skins, freeing the juice, and transfers the mass of skins and juice to a vat. Within hours, the winery is filled with a distant buzzing that increases as more vats are filled. Soon the vats are frothing as if some rabid beast were threatening to erupt from his liquid lair in a paroxysm of rage. In the placid environment of a small, enclosed cellar the noise seems otherworldly, which, in a sense, it is. It is the frenzy of yeasts reproducing, giving off carbon dioxide in amounts that can roil an immense vat of juice.

The intriguing part of this depiction, which occurs in many, but not all, parts of the Old World, is that the wine-grower did nothing about the yeasts. He or she took their existence—and salubrity—for granted. Yet virtually everywhere in the New World—California, the Pacific Northwest, New York State, Australia, and New Zealand—winemakers typically add a cultivated strain of yeasts to the mass of juice and skins called the must. It is done in Europe too, but not as universally. The cultivated yeasts invariably are strains isolated from European vineyards, which is reflected in their commercial names, such as the Burgundy or Champagne strain.

Is there something inherently superior about Old World vineyards to New in this matter of yeasts? Not at all. But age-old cultivation of vines has brought about a harmony between man and plant—the plant here being not just grapevines, but yeasts as well—that shows well how astonishing are the things that last. For centuries, winegrowers in these old vineyards have been returning the pomace, the squeezed-out cake of skins and stems, back to the vineyards as fertilizer. That from red wines, where the skins have been in contact with the fermenting juice, abounds in yeasts. Over time, certain highly localized strains are said to have emerged as dominant from this annual renewal.

Yeasts are everywhere in the world, many varieties being found in widely disparate places. In fact, the same species of yeasts are found in many vineyards around the world, with any differences arising more from climate than anything else. They float in the air and lodge on the ground. Eventually they catch on the waxy surface of the ripening grape. Some varieties have the ability to endure by transforming their essence from a vulnerable single-celled plant into spores with impermeable cell walls. It is as if the yeast curls up against an unfriendly world, awaiting a more benign day, which always comes.

When it does—usually a matter of rain and warmth—the spore transforms itself back to its original, delicate cell existence, awaiting a breeze, insect, bee, or bird to carry it to some sugary nourishment such as a ruptured grape.

Not all yeasts are beneficent to wine, which makes the lack of intervention in the old European vineyards the more amazing. If anything, there are more varieties and strains of yeasts that are deleterious to good wine, making wine taste bad or preventing an efficient and complete fermentation, than there are beneficent yeasts. Why then are these winemakers, who are acutely aware of wine science and the latest technology, so willing to court seeming disaster?

Here we come to the nature and variety of yeasts and how man, over the centuries, at first unwittingly and now knowingly, cultivated single-celled plants as well as grapevines. Scientists have divided the kingdom (or maybe it's just a duchy) of yeasts into fifteen genera (plural of genus), of which one in particular is of interest to those who mind their bellies. This is the genus called Saccharomyces, from the Greek words for sugar (*sakchar*) and fungus (*mykes*). It is this group that makes up most, although not all, of the yeasts used in bread making, beer making, and wine making. Seven species make up the genus, with names like *S. cerevisiae* (also called *ellipsoideus*) and *S. carlsbergensis*. The latter variety was named in honor of the Carlsberg beer people in Denmark, where the isolation of pure strains of yeasts was first developed.

These yeasts, the Latin names of which are tiring to eye and brain, are important if only because they allow the marveling observer to zero in on the particularities of wines and places. For example, in the Sauternes district of Bordeaux, where they seek to create sweet wines infused with the taste of noble rot (which comes from yet another fungus, *Botrytis cinerea*, which is said to exude its own type of antibiotic that hampers fermentation), the growers benefit from the presence of a species called *S. bayanus*.

This yeast doesn't come into play immediately, which is one of the fascinations of "spontaneous" fermentation: No one yeast accomplishes the entire fermentation, regardless of the type of wine. With the advent of cultured yeast strains, a vat of juice is fermented with a single strain. This is known as an inoculated vat. In a spontaneous fermentation, such as is practiced in many European wineries, fermentation proceeds like a multiple-stage rocket. Typically, the first stage of fermentation begins with so-called wild yeasts. These are to wine what weeds are to a garden, plants in the wrong place.

Wild yeasts are varieties that tend to start fermenting very rapidly, which isn't necessarily bad. But often they impart off flavors, which the winemaker strives mightily to avoid. They are alcohol-sensitive and die after the alcohol level reaches 4 percent. Winemakers would as soon not have such yeasts in their vats. So what the winemaker does is dose the must from the start with sulfur dioxide, the all-purpose yeast and bacteria inhibitor of wine. (This is the sulfite of "Contains Sulfites" now seen on every bottle of wine. Sulfur dioxide is also used at bottling as a bacteria inhibitor. It is harmless except to those with severe allergies to it.)

Wild yeasts are especially sensitive to sulfur, but they usually are stunned rather than killed outright. The winemaker doesn't want so much sulfur in the must as to inhibit the desired yeasts. He or she is buying time for them to take over. As a result, some slight fermentation can occur from these wild yeasts, especially when a vat is not overwhelmed by an inoculated yeast culture.

The second stage is by far the more powerful. This is when the real fermenting yeasts kick in. The species that predominates is *S. cerevisiae*. This is the great wine yeast and there are many strains of it peculiar to the locales where they live. But it doesn't have a high tolerance for alcohol and so it will probably die off after a wine reaches about 14 percent alcohol.

This matter of alcohol tolerance can be important for some wines. Yeasts both produce and are paralyzed by alcohol. No yeast can ferment a wine past 20 percent alcohol. Most are killed by alcohol toxicity at 17 percent or 18 percent. This is why you know that wines such as sherry and port, which are above 19 percent alcohol, have to have been fortified with a distilled spirit. They couldn't reach such an alcohol level strictly through fermentation. It's also why such wines are categorized as fortified wines.

All of which brings us back to Sauternes. Like other wines it, too, goes through its stages. But unlike other wines, Sauternes is both relatively high in alcohol (between 13 percent and 15 percent), and has a high level of residual or leftover sugar in the wine. So toward the end of the fermentation— it's also true of many sweet Loire wines—a different yeast kicks in, *S. bayanus*. It is not as sensitive to the toxic effect of alcohol as other yeasts and can therefore carry a fermentation further, should a winemaker so desire. Producers of Sauternes and Loire wines such as Quarts de Chaumes and Bonnezeaux, which are fermented to 13 percent to 15 percent alcohol, seek such assistance.

Also involved is the problem of unusually high sugar content in the juice. This is a particular problem for wines affected by noble rot, such as Sauternes and German wines of the Beerenauslese and Trockenbeerenauslese categories. Noble rot is a fungus that creates microscopic pores in the grape skin. The grape shrivels and loses much of its moisture through evaporation. What remains is the essence of the grape, very little juice, but all of the original sugar. The result is a juice with an unusually high percentage of sugar in it, as well as acidity, neither of which is lost through evaporation. The density of the juice is skewed, in the same way that salt water has a higher density than fresh water. This is a real problem for many yeasts, as they cannot handle the concentration of sugar.

As already noted, it really is the enzymes in the yeasts that perform the fermentation. But these enzymes operate within the walls of the yeast cell. The only way that anything can get to these enzymes is if they are in a solution—unless the enzymes are freed from their one-cell prison, as Buchner demonstrated. But this doesn't happen in a wine vat. The way in, therefore, is through the semipermeable cell wall or membrane. But if the sugar concentration is too great, the diffusion through the cell wall cannot occur. This is why sugar syrup is an effective preserving medium for fruits and jams. The reason is that the yeast cell is 65 percent water. When it is put into a solution with a higher density than its own, the result is like a tidal undertow. This is osmosis. The phenomenon of osmosis acts as a pressure, forcing the less-dense contents inside the yeast cell to pass through the semipermeable cell wall to the other side in an attempt to equalize the differing densities. Osmosis sucks it dry, rendering the yeast inactive, although not dead. This is what happens when yeasts confront grape juice with very high sugar content—or a sugar syrup in preserves.

But nature seems to have a loophole for every predicament. Yeasts can adapt to demands placed on them over time. This is one of the peculiarities of wine making: One variety of yeast can evolve into different strains, seemingly dependent upon their different environments. Whether the yeast really did temporarily modify because of its environment or whether it was genetically different from the start seems to be a matter of dispute among microbiologists. Whatever the truth, the strains of yeasts from Champagne, Burgundy, Bordeaux, the Rheingau, and elsewhere are different from each other in minor ways—greater or lesser tolerance to alcohol, temperature, carbon dioxide—even when they ostensibly are the same variety, usually *S. cerevisiae*. Also, some yeast varieties have less sensitivity to the pressure of osmosis, such as *S. rouxii*, which is a yeast that thrives in honey, jams, and preserves.

The grand question, given the increasing use of inoculated cultures, is whether these different strains produce different flavors in wines. And if so, how much of a difference? It is possible that various yeast varieties can impart a flavor. The most extreme instance, at least among those varieties sought by winemakers, is the yeast that helps create the taste of sherry, as well as the rare French wine called *vin jaune* in the Jura region. Although the grape varieties are different—the

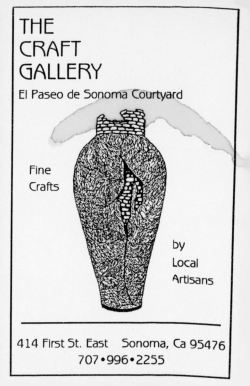

THE
CRAFT
GALLERY

El Paseo de Sonoma Courtyard

Fine
Crafts

by
Local
Artisans

414 First St. East   Sonoma, Ca 95476
707•996•2255

preponderant grape in sherry is the Palomino variety, that of *vin jaune* is Savagnin—the two wines taste similar because of a common employment of an uncommon yeast: *Torulaspora delbrueckii*.

This tongue-twister creates the phenomenon of *flor*, literally *flower*, which is a whitish film that floats on top of the wine after fermentation is complete. In time it can take on the appearance of the crinkly rind of brie cheese. In fact, it is a floating collection of reproducing yeast cells. Sherry producers had no real control over which barrels of young sherries would be visited by the *flor* yeasts and which ones, as in a Bible story, would be passed over. Those that did develop a *flor* culture were subsequently classified by the producers as *fino* sherries: they were light, delicate, and were only lightly fortified. Those passed over were baptized as *oloroso* sherries, darker, richer, and more highly fortified.

Why only some barrels of sherry nurtured a *flor* was an authentic, ages-old mystery. Now the causes are better known, although sherry producers still like to play up the serendipity of its appearance. Actually, they know pretty well which barrels of wine will cultivate the *flor* yeasts based upon the vineyard source, the time of picking, and how the wine is made. They can place wines in temperature- and humidity-controlled cellars to achieve just the right conditions to induce them, but they are loath to mention this, preferring the romance of the old—and once real—mystery of its appearance like a divine intervention in their lives. Who can blame them?

It is a wonderment. *Flor* changes the taste of the wine in an odd yet appealing way. While all sherries are intentionally oxidized, those that develop a *flor* remain pale in color due to the diminution of oxidation by the *flor* covering the wine. The yeasts impart a flavor as well. *Olorosos* are darker because they have no *flor* to protect them.

Even though sherry producers can, if they wish, predetermine which wines will develop a *flor* and which not, they still need the *flor* yeasts to create the distinctive, haunting taste of a *fino* sherry. That said, it should be pointed out that *flor* alone does not a fine *fino* make. Producers in California, South Africa, and Australia also have *flor* cultures for their sherry-style wines. Sometimes they can be very fine, sometimes not. Grapes and soil still play the informing role in wine character.

But if the so-called sherry yeast, the one used to ferment the sherries, is used to ferment other wines by means of inoculation, what are the results? Here the answer is clear. The yeast *does* impart a flavor. S. F. Hallgarten in his book *German Wines* (1976) recalls: "Many people believed that yeast would transfer the taste and flavour of its origin to the wine; for example if a French champagne yeast were to be used in a German wine, this wine would adopt some champagne characteristics. However, this is not the case. I found this to happen only once, in a Steinberger Trockenbeerenauslese which was so difficult to bring to fermentation that as a last resort sherry yeast was used. Nobody was told about this, but at the first public tasting experts considered that the Steinberger Trockenbeerenauslese had a special unusual character. There is no doubt, the sherry yeast had made its impression!"

Yeast varieties can make a difference to the taste of a wine. The question centers on the degree of difference. Relative to the quality of the fruit, it is minor. Within the context of the same juice fermented with different yeast strains of the same variety, a difference can be discerned. It is said that the red-wine strain of yeast called Pasteur will offer some additional complexity in a wine, but does not heighten the fruity taste. In comparison, some assert that the red-wine yeast from Germany called Assmannshausen brings forth the fruitiness. The white-wine yeast strain called Prise de Mousse is said to emphasize the fruitiness in white wines. Some winemakers like to use a mix of yeast strains in inoculating their vats, contending that this offers an additional complexity. Here the wheel of technology comes full circle, emulating the untampered approach of spontaneous fermentation.

Such concerns are best left to winemakers. That different strains offer different tolerances for alcohol, carbon dioxide (important for sparkling-winemakers), or sulfur dioxide is indisputable and important. But the flavor or tolerance imparted by the yeast is inconsequential compared to the flavor of the material upon which they are working: the grapes. A belief that using a Burgundy yeast strain to ferment one's Pinot Noir will result in a wine of Burgundian quality is akin to thinking that if we could wear Fred Astaire's shoes we could dance as well as he.

Flavor aside, the winemaker's dance with yeast does not end with the completion of the fermentation, which can take anywhere from one week to several months. Much depends upon temperature, the yeast variety, and the amount of oxygen and nutrients available. Eventually the fermentation will conclude, leaving behind a mass of dead yeast cells.

The sediment in a new wine can be considerable and is composed of much more than dead yeast cells. It usually contains bits of grape skins and pulp, precipitated (dropped out) proteins, even bits of stems, pips, or leaves that got into the vat. These settle out by gravity very quickly. But the dead yeast cells, being infinitely smaller, take more time to settle out. A young wine always is cloudy. With multiple "rackings"—the siphoning of clear wine from settled sediment—the wine grows progressively clearer. Most of the dead yeast cells do fall to the bottom over time. But for some wines, such as Chardonnay and above all, Champagne, the winemaker may not wish to remove these dead yeast cells with excess speed. They can impart a desired flavor by means of a phenomenon called autolysis.

Autolysis is the breakdown of the dead yeast cells by its own enzymes, releasing nitrogen, phosphoric acid, and vitamin B. Yeasts, in effect, clean up after themselves. But in the process these and other substances can aid the growth of unwanted bacteria that can lead to spoilage and off flavors.

What intrigues winemakers is that autolysis can also impart a subtle flavor flourish, particularly with white wines. In Burgundy, some winemakers like to stir up their barrels of Chardonnay with a branch pushed down through the bunghole into the barrel or, more commonly, with an eggbeaterlike device that slips through the bunghole only to unfurl like a satellite expanding its solar panels in space. The winemaker then rotates it to disperse the autolyzing, yeast-rich sediment on the bottom. This practice is controversial, as some say that it can lead to undesirable off flavors.

That autolysis can add something desirable to a wine, under the right conditions, is proved by Champagne. Here we have a clear instance of a winemaker seeking the flavors of autolysis and nobody disagreeing. In the Champagne region and everywhere else the *méthode champenoise*, or Champagne method, of making bubbles is employed, the winemaker first creates a wine that has fermented to complete dryness, or no residual sugar. This wine is left to clear and is, in fact, put through a filter to ensure that no yeast cells remain at all.

Then the *chef de caves*, or cellar master, performs the most important act in creating the quality of the Champagne, namely the blending of numerous separate batches of Pinot Noir and Chardonnay to create a blend. The blend is everything. Simply combining, higgledy-piggledy, a bunch of different Pinot Noirs and Chardonnays, no matter how good individually, will not result in a fine Champagne. This is why the *chef de caves* is the most important person in a Champagne house and the highest paid.

But autolysis can add its touch and the *chef de caves* relies on this to add a flavor flourish. The blended wine is put into the heavy bottles loved by so many. In addition a precise amount of a cultured yeast is added, plus a measured amount of sugar for the yeasts to feed on. Often the yeast strain added is Prise de Mousse because it has a high tolerance for carbon dioxide and has good flocculation qualities, i.e., it falls from the wine cleanly and in a tight mass. The bottle is tightly capped with a crown cap, as on a Coca-Cola bottle.

The Champagne method of getting bubbles in the bottle is clear proof of how yeasts can ferment without free oxygen. The bottle is tightly capped, but the yeasts can obtain oxygen from whatever might be in solution in the wine. For the Champagne winemaker this is all that's needed, as all that is wanted is the carbon dioxide given off by the yeasts in the course of their consuming the sugar. The alcohol created by the yeasts during the bubble-making process is minimal, slightly over 1 percent.

But the amount of carbon dioxide given off during the fermentation is considerable, so much so that the average Champagne bottle is under five to six atmospheres of pressure—or seventy-five to ninety pounds of pressure per square inch—from the trapped carbon dioxide. When a cork is popped from a Champagne bottle—not a good idea—it leaves the neck traveling at fifty to sixty miles per hour. I know of one Champagne lover who, sitting in her convertible Porsche, decided that it would be fun to drink some Champagne in the car. She popped the cork and, instead of flying through the open roof, it instead hit the inside of the windshield. The cork cracked the windshield.

But making the bubbles by this second fermentation, as it's known, is only part of the advantage of the *méthode champenoise*. After the yeasts die, the bottles, lying horizontally, are left to rest for years. In Champagne the minimum time is eighteen months, with the better producers leaving the wine "on the yeasts" for two years or more. A few rare bottlings, such a Bollinger RD (recently disgorged), can remain on the yeasts for six years or more.

As the wine is exposed to the autolyzing yeast cells it is subtly flavored. Technically what is going on is an increase in nitrogen compounds. According to the Bollinger technicians, the nitrogen compounds in the wine increase by about 50 percent after the wine rests on the dead yeast cells for one year, 70 percent after two years, and after six years, it is more than doubled.

To the wine drinker this is gobbledegook. Tom Stevenson, in his definitive book *Champagne* (1986) gets to the meat of the matter: "This autolytic character can be recognized in a fine Champagne of relatively youthful age by a clean yeasty aroma which, with a little more maturity, will evolve into a slightly fuller, often sweeter, bouquet reminiscent of fresh baked *brioche* paste, but the potential of a great Champagne finally emerges as a deep, mature character that is rich and has a biscuity or nutty complexity." How much of this "nutty complexity" is due to the flavoring of autolysis and how much to the maturation of the wine itself is problematic. But it is known that the longer on the yeasts, the more pronounced the character.

This same autolytic character is imparted to sherry by the *flor*. As the *flor* yeasts die, they fall to the bottom of the barrel and lie there, untouched, often for years. What makes both the sherry and the Champagne autolyses practicable, what keeps the wines from suffering otherwise likely bacterial spoilage, is that both wines are kept in unoxidized states. The Champagne is protected from oxidation and airborne contamination by the tightly sealed bottle; the *flor*-influenced sherry is protected by the *flor* layer covering the wine. Also, both wines boast unusually high levels of acidity—an effective inhibitor of bacteria—and low pH levels, which is a measurement of the force of the acidity upon the wine. The lower the pH, the greater the force of whatever acidity is present. The combination of a high level of acidity coupled with a low pH or great forcefulness is critical.

Finally, though, the winemaker has to get rid of the yeasts. The most effective means is simply to run the wine through a filter or centrifuge. The problem is that if you do this too aggressively, using filters with such tiny micropores as to take out every last yeast cell and bacterium, you also will strip the wine of its flavor. So the usual way is to let nature and gravity take its course. The winemaker will rack the wine from barrels anywhere from four to eight times over a two-year aging period. Then, depending upon the wine and the winemaker's mentality, the wine will either be lightly filtered or put directly into the bottle.

The desirability of filtering is a chafing argument in certain circles. Some connoisseurs say that any filtering removes something irretrievable from the wine and is unnecessary if the wine has been well cared for from the start. Others say that a light, gentle filtering removes little and can, in fact, be beneficial, as it attends to potentially damaging spoilage organisms that still can remain in a wine that may indeed appear absolutely limpid to the naked eye.

For what it's worth, it appears to this observer that the desirability of filtering varies dramatically with the grape variety. Tough, strong wines such as Cabernet Sauvignon, Syrah, Zinfandel, Nebbiolo, and many other red wines do not appear to be much altered by a gentle filtration. The key word here is gentle. On the other hand, Pinot Noir seems to suffer irremediably when subjected to almost any filtration. This may be more a matter of exposure to oxidation—Pinot Noir seems to bruise readily—than to the actual action of gentle filtration. In the same way, most white wines seem the better for not being filtered, although sometimes it is necessary because even the faintest cloudiness is detectable in a white wine and this is displeasing to the eye. The winemaker's obligation is to create a fine wine that transmits its message of grape, soil, and site without distortion or reduced amplitude. If filtration helps that end, then it is a good thing. If not, it should be avoided. Any sweeping condemnation of the practice, or for that matter, insistence on it, seems ill advised.

The Champagne people have a different problem: How to get the dead yeast cells out of the bottle without losing any of the bubbles? The first problem is getting the mass of dead yeast cells lying on the side of the bottle into the neck. This is accomplished by the process of riddling. Until very recently, this was always done by hand, a flabbergasting procedure in which a riddler gives each bottle a sharp, short twist or oscillation to dislodge the sediment mass and the barest tilt upward to edge it toward the neck. Keep in mind that the yeast mass is hardly cohesive. If you twist it too enthusiastically, as I once did when given the chance to try, the entire population of dead yeast cells and other bits of light and heavy sediment take off through the wine like the snow in those glass bubbles that you turn over. Settling takes another six months and the accountant gets sore. Professional riddlers, by the way, can riddle up to forty thousand bottles a day.

Now the process of riddling is increasingly handled by

mechanical devices. Riddling by hand takes about one month, the bottle being oscillated and gradually inverted once a day, to ease the sediment into the neck; the mechanical devices do it in about one week, as they can perform the operation more frequently due to greater efficiency. But on the horizon is a revolutionary method under development by the Champagne giant Moet & Chandon by which the yeasts are contained in capsules made from algae. The material of the capsules is permeable for everything the yeasts and wine need, but the dead yeast cells, even after autolysis, remain trapped in the comparatively heavy algae beads. To riddle these, all you do is invert the bottle. They fall into the neck in seconds and are caught in the little plastic cup attached to the inside of the soda-pop bottle cap already in use.

Regardless of the riddling technique, the yeasts still have to be removed without loss of bubbles. This process is called disgorgement. The old way had a highly practiced cellar worker remove the cork while holding the bottle upside down. When they say that it's all in the wrist, this is what they must have had in mind. With the bottle upside down, the worker releases the cork or cap, letting the sediment in the neck pour out. Almost simultaneously, with a twist of the wrist he flips the bottle right side up, clamping his thumb over the mouth of the bottle to prevent any clear wine from escaping. The bottle subsequently is recorked.

This ancient technique was replaced in 1891 by plunging the neck of the bottle into a freezing brine solution. In short order, the wine in the neck of the bottle freezes to a slush, entrapping the yeast cells collected there. They are then cleanly and efficiently removed by removing the cap, with no chance of loose yeasts slipping back into the bottle and destroying the clarity of the wine. All of this now is mechanized.

Regardless of whether the wine is still or sparkling, so many of the practices described in this chapter fall under the heading of technology. And technology has improved the quality of modern wines, if only by eliminating defects. But what it has not done, and what viewing wine from the perspective of yeasts so clearly demonstrates, is that nothing really has changed—except our understanding. All the fancy machines, all the shiny surfaces in today's wineries do little more than allow winemakers greater control over ancient practices. They can perform on a large scale what was once done on a smaller one: putting yeasts into grape juice to make wine—and then figuring out how to remove them.

DRINKING
WINE

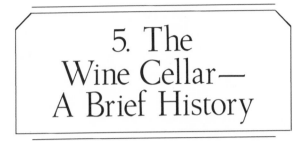

5. The Wine Cellar— A Brief History

Good wine is most frequently found among the capitalists,
who can afford to buy up large quantities in favourable
years . . . and who have a reputation to lose.

—Cyrus Redding
A History and Description of Modern Wines (1833)

The wine cellar has become something of a shrine in recent years. This is an unfortunate turn of events caused partly by the high cost of the world's rarest wines and partly by the publicity given to rich "collectors" who house these wines in lavishly appointed cellars. One can hardly blame them for buying such extraordinary wines and creating a beautiful setting for them—indeed one envies them—but it does tend to make the wine cellar seem a rare creature.

Besides, there is a substantive difference between a wine cellar that grows progressively and higgledy-piggledy from an ongoing love of wine, and the creation of a "collection." The two grow from different needs and for different reasons.

Laying down a wine, as the British so descriptively put

it, is a recent practice. Wine is several millennia old; cellaring as we know it today spans but three centuries. One cannot be categorical about this, the hedge being that we know that the ancient Greeks and Romans did drink aged wines. Various Roman authors refer to wines drunk after five, seven, fifteen, and even twenty-five years of age. A fifteen-year-old wine, one infers from such reports, was apparently not that unusual, especially in the Roman era.

Nevertheless, one must bear in mind that wine in ancient times was often unlike wine as we prize it today. Then, it was more a medium to which a multitude of ingredients were added, from such understandable additions as herbs and spices (which we still enjoy today in the woodruff-infused May Wine of Germany or with mulled wine, a warmed red wine to which nutmeg and cloves are added) to the more improbable ingredients of seawater, pitch, and resin. Pliny the Elder, writing in his *Natural History* (about 1 A.D.), goes into considerable detail as to the various qualities of pitches and resins, much in the same way that winemakers today talk about barrels made from oaks grown in different forests. The still-popular Greek wine Retsina, flavored as it is with pine resin, is practically a living fossil.

Also, we are somewhat in the dark as to the specific character of some of the ancient "wines." We don't know, for example, whether a twenty-year-old wine, referred to by one or another author, was very sweet—which is an effective preservative—or was perhaps closer to a liqueur in consistency, as in the two-hundred-year-old wine admiringly described by Pliny as "thick as honey." Aristotle observed that "the wine of Arcadia was so thick that it was necessary to scrape it from the skin bottles in which it was contained, and to dissolve the scrapings in water." The ancient Greeks, and later the Romans, frequently reduced their wines by boiling them, a practice poetically noted in Virgil's *Georgics*:

> *Or of sweet must boils down the luscious juice,*
> *And skims with leaves the trembling caldron's flood.*

This description of sweet must boiling down is not at all fanciful. In fact, it is practiced to this day in Provence at Christmas, where the creation of *vin cuit*, or cooked wine, remains a traditional seasonal practice, at least by those who have their own vineyards. Jean-Noel Escudier in his definitive 1953 cookbook on the cooking of Provence, called *La Veritable Cuisine Provençale et Niçoise* (translated by Peta J. Fuller and published in 1968 in this country under the title *The Wonderful Food of Provence*), describes the making of *vin cuit*:

> The *mout* (juice which has been pressed from the grapes but is not yet fermented) is set to cook—preferably in a copper vessel—and the froth is continually skimmed off as it rises, until the original quantity of juice has been reduced by one third. It is allowed to cool and is then carefully decanted and poured through filter paper.

In short, the vision evoked today by the word *wine* may not translate perfectly what constituted wine two or three thousand years ago.

But even if ancient wines were identical to modern, one assertion still can be made without equivocation: The history of the wine cellar began with the inexpensive glass bottle. And that moment occurred in the 1600s.

Although glass containers have sporadically been used to hold wine at least as far back as the Roman era, they were no more than a conveyance, a go-between from barrel to cup. The few wines that were transported in glass bottles were wrapped in straw or wicker not only to prevent breakage, but also because the unmolded glass was thin, bulbous, and mis-shapen. The traditional straw-covered Chianti flask, now a fading memory, was a direct descendant, right down to the woven straw base that allowed the bottle to stand securely upright.

But the great bulk of wines was shipped in barrels and consumed directly from the wood. Pure wine, unadulterated by masking flavors from herbs, spices, or honey, was not intended to be aged. Wine was largely to be drunk without a thought to a more glorious future, for there could be none.

The notion of a future for pure wine required a nonporous, inexpensive, reasonably strong container and some means of sealing it so tightly that not only would no wine leak out, but more critically, no air would seep in. The eventual marriage of the glass bottle and the cork became as heavenly a consummation as any in the history of technology.

This confluence of wine, bottle, and cork is profoundly important to our vision of what makes for good wine, as the life of a wine placed in a hermetically sealed glass cocoon is utterly different than if stored in an air-permeable barrel or cask, no matter how tightly bunged. Never before had we the experience of just how slowly or magnificently a pure wine would evolve when kept in a totally secure environment shielded from the immediate depradations of oxygen. Fernand Braudel in *Civilization and Capitalism* notes, "As late as the 18th-century a dictionary of commerce [*Dictionnaire du Commerce* by J. Savary, 1759–65] was surprised that the Romans had considered 'the age of wines as their claim to excellence, while in France wines are thought to be stale (even those from Dijon, Nuits and Orleans, the most suitable for keeping) when they reach the fifth or sixth year.' The *Encyclopédie* [1756] firmly states 'The wines of four or five years standing which some people talk of so highly are past their best.' " That said, it must be pointed out that some wine connoisseurs of the day did prefer certain wines, notably the best red Burgundies, with at least several years of age on them. Then, as now, the assessment of when a wine is at its best is in the eye and on the palate of its beholder. The authors of the *Encyclopédie* should not be thought any more definitive in such an observation than a modern observer of today's habits.

A wine that once would have soon oxidized beyond recognition or turned to vinegar (courtesy of the airborne vinegar fungus *Mycoderma aceti*) now could survive for dozens of years. In many cases nothing of interest resulted. But some wines were transformed by the opportunity and the resulting experience was like no other. Our understanding of what wine could be, of what the Earth could offer, was profoundly revised.

The inauguration of this change of vision and experience can be pinpointed to between 1620 and 1630, that moment in time witnessing a striking advance in glass manufacture. English glassblowers perfected not a cheap method of manufacture, but rather, a sturdier type of glass. This new quality of glass was thick and even throughout its shaping into a bottle (which gave it an unprecedented solidity) and was of such a dark green color as to make it appear black until held up (empty) in front of a strong light.

Naturally, such a radical change evolved over a generous span of time. The appearance of the new techniques that made possible the inexpensive glass bottle no more revolutionized either wine drinking or wine making overnight any more than a similarly radical change would today. Yet a start toward a recognition of the beauty of unsullied wine already had begun. More wine was left, for better or worse, in its natural state. Although necessarily short-lived, it was truly *veritas in vino*, to reshape that time-worn phrase a bit. Whatever its drawbacks it still was a rewarding beverage, far safer to drink than the disease-ridden water and, more important perhaps, it was a distinctive, enriching experience. Evanescent as even the best wines were, there was already present the same compelling quality, if not depth of flavor, that enabled Samuel Pepys to write in 1663, and us to understand today, his now-famous diary note about having sampled "a sort of French wine called Ho Bryan, that hath a good and most perticular taste that I never met with." One could not come up with a pithier description of Château Haut-Brion today.

Although the change from storing wine in wood to putting it in glass was not an overnight occurrence, it nevertheless gathered speed quickly. Collectors now pay dearly for good examples of those old bottles, which might reasonably lead one to conclude that they were rarities in their day. In fact, they were astonishingly abundant. By 1695 there were thirty-eight bottlehouses out of a total of ninety glassworks operating in England, with an annual production of nearly three million bottles. And this wasn't confined only to England. William Younger observes in *Gods, Men and Wine* that the movement toward bottled wine extended beyond England, pointing to what he describes as "the growing use of bottles in Bordeaux in the 1720s and 1730s and . . . the growth of glass manufactories in that region which toward 1790 turned out nearly two million bottles a year."

This instance of sizable production of bottles in Bordeaux by the end of the eighteenth century reveals the scope of the English-instigated "glass revolution." That the French recognized the English precedence was revealed by their contemporary term for the new black glass, *verre anglais*. They soon were making it themselves, despite the flattery of the name. The new English glass was either the victim of a bit of industrial espionage or its formula was independently divined by the already sophisticated French glass factories. Either way, by 1700 they were manufacturing their own *verre anglais*.

Still, there couldn't have been much laying down or cellaring of wines, at least to judge from the shape of the bottle. The original English bottles were bulbous at the base with a tall spire of a neck. Known to modern collectors as the Shaft and Globe or Globe and Spike, this was the prototype bottle crafted from the new thick, dark glass. It was free-blown, that is, without using a mold, and its shape could not have been more inappropriate for cellaring wine. This is hardly surprising, for there was no intent at the time, or for decades afterward, actually to store wine inside glass. The design was simply a sturdy, glass version of a shape that dates to the Roman era and was, in fact, used only as a decanter. The bulbous base of the Globe and Spike made laying it sideways quite difficult and the long neck made it that much harder for the wine to nestle against a cork, keeping it moist and swollen, the seal intact.

The next evolutionary phase of the English black glass bottle was the so-called Onion bottle, aptly named for its spherical shape attached to a stubby neck. It was simply the Globe and Spike slapped down a bit. Its era was incomprehensibly long, from about 1670 to 1720, incomprehensible because this time period ushered in a wine that could not but have helped abet the idea of putting a wine aside for a few years. The wine was port. Although legitimate doubt exists that port by itself caused a change in the shape of wine bottles to the point where they could easily be laid sideways, it is reasonable to presume that this rough, brandy-dosed red wine, more so than the red Bordeaux of the era, which were intentionally light, gave persuasive force to the idea of a future for wine. Given the British love of red Bordeaux, it was a twist of fate worthy of a Henry James novel.

The role played by port in helping edge the British toward purposely cellaring wine in glass to improve its drinking quality is a matter of conjecture—and not a little dispute. Because port figures so strongly as a plausible impetus for cellaring wine for its future quality, it is worthy of a slight digression to put it in the proper perspective and give it its likely due.

Toward the end of the 1600s, Britain was engaged in one of her chronic disputes with France, the result being either a series of embargoes on the wines of France (which largely meant red Bordeaux, as it was the favored drink at the time) or such prohibitive tariffs as to make French wines unavailable to all but the wealthiest.

Because of this circumstance, the red wines of Portugal soon gained an audience among thirsty, claret-deprived Britons. During the first embargo, which lasted from 1678 to 1685, shipments of Portuguese wines mushroomed from a mere 120 tuns to at least several thousand. (A tun is a cask of 252 gallons weighing about one ton when filled with wine. The capacity of modern freighters is still expressed in tonnage, the number of tuns of wine a ship could transport having originally been the determination of its carrying capacity.)

The port of that period was not precisely like that of today. Then it was a wine fortified with brandy *after* the wine was fermented, instead of brandy being added during the fermentation in order to stop it, as is done today. As a result, it was not as sweet. This sort of port did not appear until sometime after 1730. But whatever the manufacture, port is a wine that is harsh, tough, tannic, and coarse. It did not have then, nor does it have now, the "breed" of Bordeaux or its delicacy. Port is as robust as a farm dog.

By the time of the second embargo in 1689 the foothold originally gained by Portuguese wines had been lost. Sales had disintegrated in the four years between the first and second embargoes, everyone in Britain racing back to his beloved claret. But with the second embargo port sales returned, this time for good. By 1700 the average import of Portuguese wine into Britain was more than five thousand tuns and remained roughly at that level for decades afterward, as the duties on French wines remained prohibitive until 1783, when France and England signed a peace treaty.

During that long interval, port found a large audience, some of whom doubtless discovered that these coarse, tannic, and harsh red wines were smoother, more drinkable, and altogether better when kept in a sealed bottle for a while. Since their wine of preference, claret, was not to reappear in quantity until nearly the beginning of the 1800s, port wine drinkers had the opportunity of realizing the pleasing results of their (intentional or accidental) experiment in transforming a less palatable wine into a more palatable one.

As the need for the aging of port gradually made itself apparent over the decades (along with the increasing realization of what the sealed bottle meant for wine everywhere), so, too, did the shape of the wine bottle transform equally gradually from a bulbous, squat affair to something more rational for storage purposes. The beginning of this transformation is fairly easily marked at around 1740, as around that date an improved earthenware mold was created that enabled bottles to be mold-blown rather than free-blown. From this mold the first straight-sided, easily-laid-down wine bottles emerged.

The wine bottle was then under continual revision. By 1760 the body became taller with a slight taper to the neck;

by 1780 the body became taller still, the neck shorter and more cylindrical; and by 1790 the diameter of the body was reduced from five inches to three inches and the color noticeably lightened, due to an improvement in the glass itself.

But a bottle, no matter how strong and cheap, is of little long-term use to wine if it cannot be tightly sealed. Before the arrival of the now-commonplace cork, the usual practice was simply to pour a thin layer of oil on the remaining wine in a bottle to prevent dust and at least some air from penetrating. It was this replenished layer of oil, by the way, that partly accounts for our practice of having a splash of wine poured first into the host's glass. Now we are apprehensive as to a wine's condition; then it was the host's reassurance that none of the guests received an unwanted dollop of oil in his cup.

Which came first, the bottle or the cork, is one of those unsatisfying questions that is best sidestepped. Scholars have established beyond question that cork was used to seal containers of wine, and certainly a multitude of vials, flasks, and jars, at least as far back as Roman times. The lack of a strong, inexpensive, more or less standardized, nonporous container during those times made the use of cork as a closure a convenience but hardly a necessity. A plug of paper or wood or cloth was equally effective. But whatever prospects the cork may have had for more common use were brought up sharp in the Middle Ages; the idea of sealing a container with Spanish or Portuguese cork seems to have vanished during that period. But the cork was too common in Spain and Portugal to have been forgotten about completely and it needed only the arrival of a practical glass bottle to revive the long-moribund notion.

It was left to the inspired Dom Perignon, whom many credit with the creation of sparkling Champagne, to recognize not only the potential of the new glass, but also the ideal qualities of the cork as the only possible stopper. Whether he was the first to do so, as many posit, is important only to the Champagne Chamber of Commerce. His achievement was in recognizing the potential of this pairing for creating and preserving an intentionally sparkling wine. That this occurred sometime between 1670 and 1715, the year of his death, surely attests to his genius.

By 1723, according to Patrick Forbes in *Champagne: The Wine, The Land, and The People*, one contemporary witness was able to write, "Certain glass-works only make heavy glass bottles which have been in great demand ever since it was discovered that the best wines conserve better in bottle than on their lees [the sediment]." According to Forbes, by 1747 there were "no less than eleven furnaces . . . all turning out *verre anglais* bottles for Champagne." By 1785, only seventy years after Dom Perignon's death, winegrowers in Champagne were able to sell three hundred thousand bottles of sparkling wine, which prior to Dom Perignon simply didn't exist.

The importance of the glass bottle (and the cork) cannot be overestimated. The creation of inexpensive, sturdy glass bottles and the revival of the use of cork as a seal was as significant a turning point in the history of wine as the printing press was in ensuring that ideas themselves could be kept, preserved, and universally celebrated.

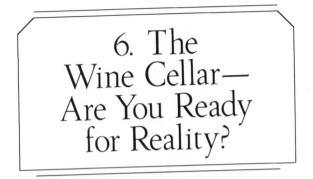

6. The Wine Cellar— Are You Ready for Reality?

If I had to live my life over again, I would try always to remember that admirable precept of Bossuet: "The greatest disorder of the mind is to believe that things are so because we wish them to be so."

—Louis Pasteur

The past few decades have seen endless discussion and argument over the effects of nature versus nurture. In a modest way, the realities of the wine cellar also center on a similar debate. How much of what happens to a wine is in the wine itself and how much is it acted upon by the cellar environment? Some wines, for example, are said not to "travel well." Wines tasted on one side of the Atlantic are thought to taste differently on the other side, despite the fact that their bottles sport the same label, vintage, and contents. How much is nature and how much nurture?

This chapter focuses on nurture: The proper conditions for a wine cellar is a subject at once complex and simple. In skeletal outline, the ingredients of a good cellar are simple: absence of sunlight and a cool temperature.

But many more precepts have been handed down to us over the centuries, encrusted with superstition and weighted with forbidding exactitude. The catechism has it that a cellar must be between fifty-two and fifty-five degrees; white wine should be stored at a cooler temperature than red; there must be no vibration; no light may be admitted; there must be an absence of any odors. The exactitude of these prescriptions is the giveaway: They trade on fear.

Bluntly put, an extraordinary amount of superstitious "wisdom" about the elements of a proper wine cellar is erroneous for the home cellar. As in so many superstitions, there is just enough truth in the assertions to make them plausible. Considerable scientific research has been performed on the subject, although not all of it is conclusive. One of the leading figures in this research is Dr. Vernon L. Singleton of the University of California at Davis Department of Viticulture and Enology, to whom I am indebted for much of the information in this chapter. At the very least, though, the subject is open to plain common sense, which I hope will soon become apparent. As my friend and colleague Alexis Bespaloff likes to say, "You'll agree for yourself."

HUMIDITY AND WINE

The purpose of a wine cellar is clear: to store wine so as to bring it to its fullest expression and thus give us that much more pleasure. Time alone would seem the sole agent, or at least the most important element, but this is not so. In fact, time is the most elastic element in the process, although it is irreplaceable. Time can be, and is, acted upon by other elements, its effects accelerated, delayed, or simply waylaid by light, heat, and cold.

Its most powerful ally, now taken for granted, is the glass bottle. A wine aged in wood—a barrel, a cask—tastes utterly different from a wine aged in a tightly sealed glass bottle. The effects of time will slow to a crawl when wine is encased in a tightly sealed glass bottle and march briskly when the wine is housed in wood. With respect to the home cellar this fact would seem to be of academic interest, as cellaring wine in a barrel is now the exclusive province of the winery or shipper. But not so long ago many consumers bought their wine by the barrel and bottled it themselves.

This distinction between what happens to wine in a wooden barrel and what transpires in a near-hermetically sealed glass bottle is critically important. This is because much of the hand-me-down wisdom about the necessary conditions for a proper home cellar is wisdom only for wine held in wood.

It commonly is held that an ideal cellar should retain a considerable humidity. Without citing who said what (the list of authoritative admonitions as to exactly what degree of humidity is impressive), suffice it to say that the conventional wisdom demands that a good cellar have about 70 percent humidity. Some observers recommend as much as 95 percent humidity. One hears of how cellar floors are covered with sand and sprinkled with water from time to time so as to ensure a high humidity. This is a common practice in numerous European wineries. Expensive temperature-controlled wine cabinets for apartment dwellers go to expensive lengths to ensure a constant, precise humidity. The humidity is necessary, goes the conventional thinking, in order to keep the cork moist.

But how important is humidity in a home cellar? French and especially British wine cellars are naturally humid, given the maritime and continental climates those two nations endure. Any Parisian with a sinus problem can attest to the humidity in Paris during the winter and surely Britain needs no further examination of its well-known clime. This sort of humidity lends itself wonderfully to fungus growths, which give us those terribly ancient-looking wine cellars. Part of the long-standing insistence on humidity in the cellar is no doubt due to the fact that these traditional cellars are humid and wines certainly keep well in them.

The inevitability of such humidity does not, however,

account for its desirability. That may be better explained by the needs encountered when holding wines in wood. Before the advent of château or estate bottling of wines, it was common for wine to be shipped and held in wooden barrels or casks, even in private homes and certainly in restaurants. Private consumers bottled their own wines when they saw fit. Moreover, it was common in the 1800s and the early part of this century for a wine to be aged in wood intentionally for four or six years or even more before being bottled. This still is done in some parts of Spain and Portugal, as they like the taste of wood and the oxidation it accommodates.

The wooden barrel, unlike glass, is porous. This is a compelling fact to a shipper holding hundreds of thousands of gallons of wine in barrels in his cellars. In such circumstances one most definitely wants a high humidity, which helps keep the staves tight, the wood moist (even when empty), and ultimately reduces the amount of evaporation through the pores of the wood. Even in a fairly humid cellar about 10 percent of the contents of a barrel is lost through evaporation every year. One can only wonder what the rate might be in desertlike conditions.

But the precept that a home cellar should be humid is a relic of the past, or at least an inappropriate carryover from a different cellaring situation. A bottled wine spends its life in an utterly different environment, one impervious to moisture or humidity-laden air.

What about keeping the cork moist? Think about it for a moment. A good cork creates a near-hermetic seal in a bottle. One end of it is kept downright wet by the wine, assuming the bottle is laid on its side. The sides of the cork are surrounded by glass, to which the cork adheres with a barnaclelike grip. This is achieved because once the cork is cut into its familiar cylindrical shape, the numerous individual cells, like polyps forming a coral reef, are sliced open. They become miniature suction cups when the cork is rammed into the neck of the bottle. (Cork is a closed-cell structure with forty million cells per cubic centimeter, each filled with shock absorbers.

It can be compressed to half its size yet recover its original dimensions within hours.) This is why air cannot seep between the cork and the neck of the bottle. Only when the cork is dislodged and the suction ruptured can air slip past the cork. Air cannot pass through the cork itself.

Since the seal of the cork in the bottle is practically airtight, whatever moisture is present in the air can only affect the topmost layer of the cork, just as the wine itself affects a surprisingly small portion of the cork next to it. We know that even when wet, cork is only slightly absorptive. This is easily demonstrated by slicing off a thin layer of the wine-exposed end of a cork protecting a red wine. The wine penetrates the cork hardly at all.

The surface area of the end of the cork exposed to the air is so small as to be utterly inconsequential. Moreover, it is covered by lead or plastic in which a few tiny airholes are punched. These capsules (coverings) are recent. Until this century, the most common cork covering was a thick layer of wax, which is impermeable by air. And the ancient corks on these old bottles still triumph in sealing the bottle.

There even is serious doubt as to whether it is necessary to lay the bottles on their sides to keep the cork moist. Not all wines traditionally are treated so. In addition to the rare bottles of Tokaji Eszencia from Hungary, which are stored standing up, it was and still is common practice in the Piedmont area of Italy to place bottles of Barolo and Barbaresco in an inaccessible part of the cellar they call the *infernot*. The wines are always stored standing up, often in vertical niches carved out of the rock walls of the cellar. I can attest from personal experience that the corks and the wines appear no different from old wines stored horizontally.

More scientific evidence to this effect has been presented by the Long Ashton Research Station in England. A comparative experiment with wines stored horizontally and vertically revealed that, at least after two years of storage, "no significant differences" were found between the differently treated wines, save one: the corks in vertically stored wines were far more difficult to extract, requiring some hundred pounds of pull compared to twenty-five pounds of pull needed for the horizontally stored bottles. This only confirms what Professor Ribereau-Gayon of the University of Bordeaux discovered in a similar experiment he performed in 1931. An ongoing experiment with sparkling wine at Domaine Chandon in Napa Valley so far reveals that the cork-up position offers what they describe as a "dramatic reduction in the incidence of 'pegged' corks [compressed, nonresilient corks that are permanently molded to the shape of the bottle neck], and improved 'mushroom' shape of the standard cork after removal and improved cork appearance."

Although it is true that the cork does not provide a true hermetic seal, it comes very close to that state of airtight perfection. Just how tight is demonstrated by sparkling wines. Here we have an abundance of carbon dioxide, so much so that six atmospheres of pressure are exerted upon both bottle and cork, about the same pressure as you'd find in the tire of a bus. But the seal achieved by the cork is such that even with this pressure, the wine loses its sparkle only very gradually. Even old bottles of sparkling wine, upwards of twenty-five years of age, still retain much of their sparkle with the original cork still in place after all those years.

That the seal is not absolute is revealed by the baffling occurrence of what is known as ullage, whereby wine is lost from an old bottle in which the cork still is apparently intact and no obvious leakage is evident. The degree of the ullage, or loss, is described based on the level of the wine in an upright bottle: high shoulder, mid-shoulder, or low shoulder. Often, but not always, wines with no more ullage than high or mid-shoulder still can taste appropriate for their age, no more oxidized than a completely full bottle.

How can this be? How can wine get out and air not get in? The answer lies in the size of molecules that can slip past the sides of the cork. What is being lost is water. Wine is 70 percent to 80 percent water. While molecules of water can eventually make their way past an aging cork that slowly is losing some of its resilience, oxygen molecules are nearly twice the size of water molecules. While one can get out, the other still can't get in. It also explains why ullaged wines usually retain the same amount of alcohol as they had when young: ethyl alcohol molecules are twice the size of water molecules. They can't get out either. But even this degree of molecular slippage requires decades of aging before a good cork begins to loosen its grip even to this extent, let alone giving way altogether.

Humidity in the home cellar is an irrelevancy. It also can be a nuisance, encouraging as it does lush growths of mold and fungus. But the humid cellar has given us one benefit: The "branded" cork, which has the name of the château or estate inked onto the side, along with the vintage and, if necessary, the individual vineyard.

Not long after labeled bottles of wine were stowed in humid British and French cellars, in the 1800s, it became apparent that one could not read the labels for the mold, assuming even a shred of the label still was clutching the bottle. This remains commonplace in some French restaurants and even wine shops. Anyone lucky enough to have visited the three-level cellar of Paris wine merchant Jean-Baptiste Besse has discovered in that humid subterranean empire the enological equivalent of an elephant burial ground. A great stack of wine bottles lie resting, piled on top of each other with abandon, the labels of all of them eaten away by humidity, mold, and fungus.

With luck, one can read the brand through the neck of the bottle after removing the capsule. A number of port producers, recognizing from the outset that no label would stand up to multiple decades of aging in a British cellar, discarded paper labels altogether, preferring to paint the name of the wine onto the bottle itself. The practice is continued to this day.

The branded cork also lent itself to establishing authenticity. A staggering amount of fraud was common in the wine business during the late 1800s and the early 1900s, from shippers to importers to merchants to restaurateurs. Although fraud has been common to wine for ages, it took on new dimensions in this period due, in large part, to the desperate effects of the phylloxera plague, in which a root louse accidentally brought from America wiped out the entire European winefield in the last third of the nineteenth century. The degree of the ensuing fraud was a major reason for the emergence of château or estate bottling, as famous and precious names were being usurped with unparalleled audacity.

Unscrupulous merchants and, especially, restaurateurs, were not above switching labels on wines, pasting a famous label on a bottle of wine they had filled with Château Swill or simply soaking the label off a lesser wine and giving it a new identity. Often the bottle would be uncorked prior to its arrival at the table.

As a result of such shenanigans, we now have the elaborate ceremony of the presentation of the cork. We are given the cork not to smell, but to read. There is nothing to be learned by smelling the cork, any more than there is to be gathered about the quality of a shoe by smelling the sock. The sommelier smells the cork because it gives him something to do. The silver cup or *tastevin* hanging from a chain around his neck is not supposed to be decorative, although it too often is. It should be used to taste the wine before serving it, as that's the only way he or she, like you, will know whether or not the wine is sound.

Humidity has proved to be the inadvertent handmaiden to authenticity. In that one regard, it has proved useful in the home wine cellar.

VIBRATION, MOVEMENT, AND WINE

It is necessary to distinguish between vibrating wine and moving it, as the two are not at all identical. For present purposes, one might define vibration as a tremulous, jittery effect on wine and movement as a great sloshing about.

There is a sizable body of centuries-old wine wisdom related to the effects of vibration on wine, overwhelmingly weighted on the side that contends that continual or chronic vibration is deleterious. Vibration is thought to "tire" the wine, with the result that it ages prematurely.

A good summing up of the hoary thinking on the matter appears in Bordeaux wine shipper Edouard Kressmann's 1968 book *The Wonder of Wine*, translated from the French:

> A cellar should be situated in a calm place. Wine cannot well stand the traffic in the street, the proximity of a railway or subway line or simply some motor or other: they cause vibrations which disturb the wine, supposedly sleeping in the calm of its cellar. Such vibrations, though they may be imperceptible to our senses, in time produce a phenomenon similar to that resulting from a journey. It seems that the effect of vibration on wine has not yet been subject to deep investigation. It is merely known that it exists and that it gives rise to an active and tireless aging.

Kressmann's father, in the late 1920s, was sufficiently curious about the accelerated aging possibilities of vibration on wine that he pressed his son into the unenviable task of attempting to induce the then-unsalable 1928 vintage to soften up a bit.

> My father believed that he had discovered that the shorter the wave-length of the vibrations, the more effective was the aging. He then had the idea of having a long cylindrical receptacle made of bronze, with a ring at one end. This receptacle was filled with wine, of which he kept a sample separately. The cylinder was hung up, and was beaten like a bell with metal "clapper." He had invented a name for this process: aging by "concussion."

This bronze bell was filled with the recalcitrant 1928 vintage and the result, Kressmann ruefully notes, was that "in vain did I beat the bell for hours on end, there were no more than paltry results to get out of it." The experiment was subsequently abandoned.

It seems so plausible that wine can be somehow fatigued by vibration. After all, wine is a living thing, goes the refrain. It takes little enough imagination to make the necessary anthropomorphic leap. The identification is so tempting that even the most rational among us find ourselves beguiled by the notion. But is it true?

The research of Dr. Singleton and others reveals that the effect of vibration *alone* on wine is of no consequence, at least until the phenomenon of "cavitation" is reached. This is an extreme situation in which a void created within a liquid subsequently collapses. The pressure and temperature created by this momentary but monumental action are profound: The pressure is thought to be on the order of millions of atmospheres and the temperature to be at least 18,000 degrees Fahrenheit. The vibration necessary to cause cavitation in a bottle of wine, one may be sure, is far removed from everyday life.

Not everyone, it might be noted, scurried from a trembling locale. Turn-of-the-century London wine importers frequently housed their barrels of wine under railway arches, confident that the vibrations set forth by overhead trains speeded the maturity of the wines, or at least aided in settling the sediment.

It is possible that vibration, if sufficiently severe, could affect the sediment in a wine, although it is doubtful that it was in any way helpful to merchants storing row upon row of barrels. Most certainly it failed to accelerate the aging of it in any way, or harm it either.

According to Dr. Singleton, who has specialized in the effects of vibration on wine, "The only bad feature about vibration is possibly in dispersing sediments. You may, if you disperse them hard enough and often enough, find that it produces such fine particles that it fails to settle. So it may affect clarity, which in turn, can affect flavor. But barring that, I can say that vibration doesn't make a difference. If you can look at a bottle of wine and it's still clear, then it wasn't vibrated enough to make a difference."

This is the nub of the matter: When vibration becomes so severe that there is actual and considerable movement of the wine itself, vibration may be a legitimate concern. A minor vibration, according to Dr. Singleton's research, is of no consequence, no matter how continuous. Those who have been advised not to install an air conditioner in a closet for fear that the vibrations of the unit would harm the wine by accelerating its maturation may skip happily to their local installer. The maintenance of a steady coolness will be the sole result (along with a higher electric bill) and one's wines will mature as they should.

But what about moving a wine? Wine journals are filled with stories about the quality of wines that taste miraculously fresh because the bottles have not been moved from a cellar for decades. Movement of wine has been subject to a good deal of speculation and illogical conclusions over the centuries. Typically, it has been thought to speed the aging of wine, independent of the effects of heat. There is the well-known legend of the miller, who, lacking well-aged wine for his daughter's wedding feast, attached small barrels of wine to the arms of his windmill and was thus able to serve aged wine to his guests a few days later. Surely all they got was an oxidized wine, due to the heat of the day, and a cloudy wine to boot, the sediment having been thoroughly tumbled by then.

The most famous example of wine thought to age prematurely because of movement is that of barrels of wine put aboard sailing ships. Barrels of wine traditionally were stowed as ballast aboard ships sailing from Bordeaux. Particularly hard, tannic wines were used and it was frequently discovered that when the ships returned from the Indies or wherever, the wine was miraculously drinkable. In fact, it was fully mature in taste. It was commonly concluded that the rocking of the wines due to ocean swells speeded its maturation.

Theories of agitation or movement as a maturing agent were once so widespread and given such credence that a number of patents were issued in France during the latter half of the 1800s for mechanical devices. One device resembled a butter churn; another had the entertaining notion of fabricating a small circular railway with wavy rails. Barrels were to be placed in little railcars and a little train would circumnavigate, unsteadily to be sure, on the wavy rails. The "molecular state" of the wine was supposed to have been changed according to the patent.

In almost every instance in which movement or agitation of wine has been thought to age it prematurely, the wine has been in wood. Leaving aside the most probable cause of premature aging, heat, wine in a wooden container is that much more likely to be oxidized if jostled, especially if the container is only partly full and thus has a generous airspace at the top.

But wines stored in tightly sealed glass bottles are not subject to oxidation except in the slowest possible manner. Can a bottle of wine be harmed simply by agitating it? Does a bottle of wine that has never been moved taste better than another bottle that has been shifted, transferred, or transported?

"It's entirely possible," replies Dr. Singleton. "But you've got to consider the wine and the circumstances. Vibration we know to be of virtually no consequence, but movement is another thing. It's like shaking it up. And that may either temporarily, or, if it's sufficiently violent, permanently produce a haze. The clearest example is if you decant a bottle of wine that has a sediment and then taste what's left behind. You know that it can often be quite unattractive, harsh, and bitter. So dispersing the sediment can, possibly, change the flavor of the wine."

The potential for altering the quality of a wine by dispersing the sediment is a sometime thing, Dr. Singleton concedes. We do know that old wines are fragile and, of course, well-made old wines do contain larger amounts of sediment than do younger bottles. Alteration in taste remains a possibility, but not even a likelihood, unless the sediment fails to settle and remains in suspension. Besides, not all sediment is distasteful. In fact, older wines lacking sediment because of enthusiastic filtration tend not to be as fine as those filtered only slightly or not at all. And if sediment is so inimical to the flavor of the wine, then surely it would taint the wine simply by being in the same bottle with it? Movement of wine, in and of itself, is of little import, even for wines with sediment.

Rather, the key element about movement is much more likely to be the potentially adverse conditions associated with moving a bottle of wine. "Movement in the sense of cashing a wine, shipping it by truck, rail, plane, or ship *can* lead to negative effects on an old bottle of wine," notes Dr. Singleton, "because it is inevitably associated with temperature changes and that, in turn, can involve cork movement. If the cork is fragile for some reason, which is quite likely in an old bottle of wine, it could be easily dislodged by temperature fluctuations, thus letting wine get out or air get in."

In theory, I enquired of Dr. Singleton, if an old bottle of wine filled with sediment was placed in a temperature-controlled container straight from the cellar in such a way as to not disturb the sediment (upright, for instance), would it taste any different from another bottle that never left the cellar?

"I'll bet there isn't an expert in the country," countered Dr. Singleton, "who could tell one bottle from another still in the original cellar. And if they did, it was probably a difference between bottles before it left."

WINE AND TEMPERATURE

The very notion of a cellar implies a concern about temperature and, more specifically, a concern about excessive heat. Otherwise, we would all be hearing about famous wine attics or sunrooms. The cellar was chosen long ago for the not-so-simple reason that it offered, with no further alterations, the desirable ingredients of space, darkness, and above all, a steady, stolid, beneficent coolness. Summertime arrives and a traditional old cellar rouses itself only grudgingly, raising its temperature slowly and by miserly degree. It responds to the cold of winter with similar reluctance. For a wine, no better guardian could be appointed.

A cellar is ideal only because it is an inherently cheap means of providing wine the cool and steady temperature it responds to best. A cave is even better, as shippers in the Loire Valley who capitalize on the abundant natural caves of the area can well attest. But it is by no means the only possible storage area and its attributes can be replicated with greater or lesser success in other parts of the home. (City apartments, with their limited space and relentless steam heating and central air conditioning, do seem to be especially vexing, though.)

No matter where a wine is stored, its future is determined by the temperature of its surroundings. Here the accumulated lore of wine has become more specific, identifying "ideal" temperature ranges for red, white, and sparking wines. In no instance are such recommendations injurious. If anything, they are admirable and experience has borne them out to be, indeed, ideal.

But the categorical quality of such instructions is enough to give any wine lover the willies. What will happen to my wines if my cellar (or closet or cupboard) is 62 or 70 degrees rather than the requisite 55 degrees? And what if the temperature fluctuates 10 degrees between daytime and nighttime? Winter and summer?

The answers are neither as exact nor as definitive as the original prescription. Rather, the answers lie in an understanding of the effects of heat and cold upon wine, the effects of their fluctuation, and a recognition of the intended effect of a fairly cool environment.

WINE AND HEAT

Compared to the impact of heat upon wine, it may be fairly (if broadly) said that no other influence is of any importance, assuming the seal, i.e., a good cork, is intact. If kept away from heat, a bottle of wine can withstand the assault of just about anything (short of oxygen) and still come out smelling even better than a rose, ideally like La Tâche or Château La Mission-Haut-Brion or pretty much whatever it's supposed to smell (and taste) like. But heat can be its undoing, or can at least speed it to a lopsided sort of "maturity" which bespeaks greater time in the bottle than actually occurred.

The role of heat upon wine has been thoroughly investigated, at least with respect to its initial impact. Curiously, there has been much less investigation of the ability of wine to recover from the trauma. Some exploration of this has recently been undertaken, with a gratifying conclusion: It can recover somewhat, although never to return to its state prior to its encounter with high heat. This underscores the paradoxical notion that fine wine is at once fragile and remarkably tough. In this respect wine is not unlike fine crystal, as anyone can attest who has heart-stoppingly dropped a Baccarat glass on the floor only to discover that it did not—this once—shatter.

The effect of heat upon wine has been recognized and toyed with at least since the Roman era and quite likely in ancient Greek times as well. Roman amphorae of wine were sealed with plaster and placed in the sun. More manipulative was the practice, common since 120 B.C. according to one French historian, of hanging a gum-lined, plaster-sealed jar of wine in the chimney or over a smoking fire. Eventually the practice became frequent enough that special rooms, called *fumaria*, were constructed to accommodate a large number of containers of wine to be heated. Although it is frequently asserted that the Romans savored the smoky quality the fire imparted to the wine, which they no doubt did, the record is clear that they also recognized and sought the effect of heat upon the wine. The Romans liked aged wines.

The effect of the heat, then as now, was that the wine tasted more mature, rounder, richer, fuller, more like an older wine. It brings out the characteristics, if not the character, of a mature wine.

The maturation of aging of wine, at its most elemental level, is a matter of chemical reactions. This makes wine sound unappealing, but it is, after all, just another solution to a chemist. For the wine lover, conceding wine to be just another solution in which chemical reactions occur is useful, if only because it is the key to understanding what transpires in the dark of one's cellar, closet, or cupboard.

The effect of heat upon wine follows a pattern commonly found in many other solutions, namely that heat accelerates the chemical reactions. Heat speeds up the molecules in the wine. These collide, create a form of energy, and thus activate other molecules. What results is what is commonly referred to as a chemical reaction.

When you apply heat to a wine two conditions result: You lose fruitiness and grapiness and you gain bottle bouquet and aged character. You can go from pleasant and grapey to blah and uninteresting simply by heating a wine in the absence of oxygen, in other words, in a bottle.

When a wine is exposed to heat two conditions result: You lose freshness and fruitness. You gain heightened scent —known as bottle bouquet—and a greater roundness in taste, at the expense of freshness. The ideal is bottle bouquet *and* freshness. That takes time and a cool temperature.

Heating a wine, or simply storing a bottle at warmer temperatures, will bring about this bottle bouquet that much faster, but at the expense of a fresh, fruity taste. The result is often similar to wines that have been overaged in wood barrels, like some Spanish Riojas or old-style Italian Barolos, in which a rapturous fragrance is lofted over a rickety, insubstantial body of taste. The wine is bereft of fruit; it is more a ghost than a life, sensed but not felt.

Curiously, cold has little or no deleterious effect on the development of wine until it reaches the freezing point, which for wine is about 27 degrees Fahrenheit. Cold only slows down the rate of chemical reactions, an effect most pithily recognized in a well-known (to chemists) equation called the Arrhenius equation. A Nobel Prize–winning Swedish chemist around the turn of the century, Svante August Arrhenius bequeathed to the world the observation that if you have an increase of 18 degrees Fahrenheit you should double the rate of the average chemical reaction. The same holds true in reverse: the colder, the less the rate of reaction. Technically, the "coefficient" of this rate of increase is between 1.5 and 3, but the rule of thumb is to double the reaction rate. But this measure, a wine stored at 55 degrees will age twice as fast when stored at 73 degrees.

With this in mind we now arrive at a contemplation of the "ideal" temperature for storing a wine. We want a wine to emerge from the cellar filled with a fresh-tasting fruitiness, yet largely devoid of tannin and proffering a memorable range of scents and aromas. But we would like to experience this within our lifetime, preferably more than a few times for more than a few of the great vintage years of our time. Patience is one thing, inhumanly delayed gratification is quite another. Vintage port for the British, according to P. Morton Shand writing in 1929 in *A Book of Other Wines Than French*, is "rightly considered unequalled as the test of the pretensions of a county family to proper pride, patient manly endurance, Christian self-denial, and true British tenacity. The grim struggle," he recounts, "is fought to a sporting finish in a couple of generations or so, though the gamest and biggest wines see out father, son, and grandson, each of whom dies in peace of mind knowing he leaves a fair field to his successor after having played out his life in the straight game as a clean amateur sportsman and an honourable English gentleman."

The spiritual element of cellaring aside, the object obviously is to achieve a golden mean between suitable time in the bottle for the unfolding of bottle bouquet and reduction of tannin and some sort of reasonable dispatch. The naturally occurring European cellar temperature of around 55 degrees Fahrenheit has proved to be just such a golden mean. Wines neither matured too rapidly at that temperature nor deteriorated alarmingly fast. A wine could achieve substantial bottle bouquet while losing its fruitiness only gradually.

But 55 degrees is an arbitrarily chosen temperature. Wines stored at lower temperatures (short of freezing) simply will take longer to arrive at the desired state. Wines stored at higher temperatures will prove ready to drink that much sooner. Where the cutoff point is at the higher temperatures— when the wine rapidly loses its fruitiness in exchange for an equally rapid acquisition of bottle bouquet—is problematic.

Part of the difficulty in establishing the highest desirable temperature rests with the fact that every type of wine responds to temperature slightly differently. Which explains the truth of the traditional precept that white wines should ideally be cellared at lower temperatures than reds, say around 50 degrees.

A cold temperature, as Arrhenius demonstrated, will reduce the rate of reaction. Cellars of exceptional coldness, such as are found in the caves of the Loire Valley and the deep chalk cellars of Champagne, can preserve the freshness and fruitiness of the delicate white wines grown in those regions for an astonishingly long time. The high acidity of these wines also is instrumental. Bottles of undisgorged Champagne can lie in the chalk cellars of that northerly locale for decades and retain not only an extraordinary measure of fresh fruitiness, but even a noticeable degree of effervescence, despite the onslaught of thirty or forty years. Even in the case of naturally durable red Bordeaux, the cellars of the great Scottish estates are famous for coughing up miraculously well-preserved examples of wines as old as a century. Anyone who has shivered through a Scottish summer can well imagine what their winters must be like, let alone a deep cellar in such a climate.

What we value in white wines is precisely what such low year-round temperatures preserve: fresh fruitiness. The absence of tannins in white wines renders them more vulnerable to oxidation. Tannins help protect a wine against oxidation because they use the oxygen molecules in the wine to bond the tannin molecules in longer chains. The oxygen is thus bound up by the tannins and cannot readily respond to the stimulus of heat. Heat can cause oxidation only if oxygen molecules are available to be excited.

But what about fluctuation in temperature? Only the very deepest cellars will not fluctuate somewhat from daytime to nighttime and winter to summer. Fluctuating temperatures, especially when the swings are wide, are thought to "tire" a wine, speeding it to an early dissolution.

There is little question that oscillating temperatures *do* affect a wine adversely. But the harm to the wine is due not to the fluctuation of temperature per se but to its movement in the higher heat range. Whether a cellar temperature fluctuates from 40 degrees to 50 degrees, day to night or even hour to hour, is simply not going to make much of a difference to the wine.

But when temperatures fluctuate toward the higher range, then the wine is subject to the effects of heat. How long it must remain exposed to a higher heat for the wine to register a reaction that we can perceive depends on how high the temperature and how long it persists. The higher the heat, the shorter the time necessary for it to take a toll. Since cold doesn't affect wine negatively, short of freezing, and a moderate 55 to 65 degrees is desirable, then the spectrum of what constitutes undesirable high heat really *begins* at about 70 degrees. At that temperature and beyond, the rate of chemical reactions really begins to increase; the rate of reaction is geometric.

This helps explain why it is asserted that certain young wines, especially delicate white wines such as Muscadet, do not "travel well." It is related to similar reaction curves. Much of the character of wines that are intentionally fermented at very low temperatures, what is known as cold fermentation, comes from the presence and retention of esters, which the technique helps retain in the wine.

Esters are sweet-smelling compounds created both in the grape and from reactions between the acids and the alcohol of wine as it matures. They are responsible for much of the scent of a wine and are extremely sensitive to heat and oxidation. So, for example, the idea that certain wines can taste great in a cellar in France and not so great in New York may be attributable to ester loss.

Temperature fluctuation *can* cause a problem: cork movement. As every physics teacher has pointed out, liquids are relatively incompressible. But air expands and contracts with changes in temperature. If a bottle of wine was filled to the cork, a rise in temperature would force what little air is trapped inside to expand. Since the wine is not about to compress, then something has to give, namely the cork. Wine producers are well aware of this and they take care to leave a limited space between the wine and the cork to accommodate the expansion. But some wines, especially white wines, which are more susceptible to the deteriorating effects of oxygen, can be topped up quite close to the cork. It takes only a brief swing through a high temperature to dislodge the cork, with the possibility that air can seep into the wine along the sides of the cork until the resilience of the cork reseals the bottle. If the cork has lost its resilience, for whatever reason, then the seal may not re-form at all or imperfectly so.

Temperature change from warm to cold can create a vacuum, pulling the cork inward, but this is less likely to be as forceful as expansion. Much more common is the effect of expansion from cool to warm, with the effect of the cork bulging beneath the capsule, like a lava dome building in a volcano. Whether the wine is harmed is another matter; much depends upon how insulting the temperature and how long its duration, as well as whether the cork reseated itself quickly. Temperature fluctuation, in and of itself, is meaningless unless it involves high heat—which wreaks its own damage—or movement of the cork.

Although it is apparent from research that exposure to high heat, even briefly, can accelerate the aging of a wine disproportionately, the prospect of a summertime heat wave need not leave the wine lover sobbing on a friend's shoulder or wringing her or his hands pitifully. Much depends upon the highest temperature achieved and how long it lasts. It does take a while for a temperature change to penetrate a room and then a glass bottle, especially if the wines are kept in their cardboard or wood boxes (both are good insulators).

Also, much depends upon the wines themselves. A critical element is high acidity. Wines retaining high levels of acidity, which means good-vintage Chardonnays, Pinot Noirs, Nebbiolos, Cabernet Sauvignons, Sauvignon Blancs, and others, are less likely to react immediately to heat. Tannic wines will respond much less readily than those lacking tannin, such as older red wines or white wines.

Barring an extreme situation—very high heat for weeks at a time—the worst that likely will happen is that the wine will lose fruitiness and gain a precocious bottle bouquet. One of the inquiries of the Long Ashton Research Station involved the effects of very high heat—80 degrees and 95 degrees Fahrenheit—on red and white wines exposed to these two heat levels for six weeks. "A wide range of wines—from Champagne to German wines to claret to sherry to simple branded wines" were subjected, according to the report. These were compared to another batch that were left in a wine shop for the same six weeks during a "typical English summer with no long spell of warm weather." Triangular tastings (three samples, two of which are the same in order to assess the consistency of the tasters) were performed. The results showed that the wines subjected to the high temperatures revealed "very little tastable difference," although the white wines did suffer "a little more" than the reds. What changes were discernible were exclusively those associated with oxidation. Two wines did deteriorate at the high temperatures: Barsac (a sweet wine from the Sauternes district) and Champagne. Both darkened in color and were noticeably oxidized.

A unique aspect to Dr. Singleton's research on the effects of very high heat upon wine had to do with how well the wine *recovered* from its ordeal. After subjecting wines to blistering temperatures for an extended period Dr. Singleton reports that "to a degree the wine did recover. And although it didn't regain fruitiness, it did gain some apparent age. It was rather pleasant."

It might be said that wine resembles the mythological Icarus, whose wax wings carried him perfectly millions of miles to the sun, only to melt as he drew closer to the heat. So it can be, distressingly, with fine wine. But like Icarus, you've got to go the distance first.

WINE AND LIGHT

"Darkness is all" sayeth the lords of cellaring. As with the general precept that a wine is best off where it is cool, there is no disputing that an absence of light can only benefit a wine. But again, this precept has been handed along unblinkingly, as it were, without regard for whether the light in question is natural sunlight or the newfangled artificial light. The effects of the one are not necessarily conveyed by the other.

As far as wine is concerned, light involves more than what the human eye can perceive. We cannot, for instance, perceive the extreme blue end of the light spectrum called ultraviolet, yet a wine, like a dog hearing a "soundless" dog whistle, can respond to its impulses.

The effect of light upon wine is determined not only by what wavelengths are involved but, far more importantly, the intensity of the light. A weak light of whatever wavelength is far less likely to take a toll than a strong beam, as anyone who has tried to get a tan on a beach during the winter months can attest.

The only light that mattered prior to the twentieth century was sunlight. No candle, gas lamp, or kerosene lamp could give off the degree of intensity necessary to affect a wine the way even a bit of sunlight could. So, as with the matters of humidity and vibration, much of the concern about darkness and wine is founded upon concerns of the past.

The effect of sunlight upon wine is hardly unimportant today, as bottles of wine can frequently be found in many merchant's sun-filled windows or upon the sunlit shelves of the wine drinker at home. Wine producers are aware of the possible, even likely, abuse of wines in this manner and a considerable research has been undertaken to investigate the effects of various wavelengths of light upon wines and practical means of preventing harm to a wine from these effects.

The effect of sunlight upon wine is straightforward. A "sunstruck" wine is oxidized. (The ultraviolet end of the spectrum is particularly injurious, as oxygen absorbs this wavelength.) Often, the color of the wine is degraded, red wines becoming reddish-brown and white wines browning outright. A wine can take on a sharp, vinegarlike smell as volatile acids increase. Tannins in a wine can drop out, leaving a once-tannic red wine debilitated.

The molecules in a wine are excited or activated by being hit with a sufficiently intense beam of radiant energy. Different molecules are affected by different wavelengths of light, which complicates things immensely for the scientist attempting to unravel which wavelength affects what.

As a result of being excited by this form of energy, the molecules dance, creating heat or chemical reactions that are not heat-related. But as Louis Pasteur discovered a century ago, heat, whether from radiant energy or another source, has little or no effect upon wine—at least for brief amounts of time—as long as there is no molecularly free oxygen in the bottle. This explains why some methods of pasteurization have surprisingly little effect upon wine when the heat is applied in an atmosphere devoid of oxygen, such as a vat that is flushed with nitrogen or carbon dioxide to drive out the oxygen and then sealed tightly.

Sunlight hitting a bottle can have its way with wine, providing one or another wavelength can get through the glass. If the bottle is clear (which is common with Sauternes), it offers little defense against even the most timid sunbeam. An experiment performed in 1941, involving various wines stored in clear glass bottles that were filled completely, showed that the wines were able to withstand exposure to sunlight for as long as two months without noticeable change. However, if there was any airspace at all in the bottle or if the time period went beyond two months with the completely filled bottles, then sunlight proved itself harmful. Browning ensued, tannins precipitated, red pigments in the red wines were degraded, and volatile acidity increased. Equally enlightening was a sideline study that had the same wines stored away from sunlight, but at a temperature of 85 degrees Fahrenheit. Storage at this temperature resulted in similar, but less drastic changes.

Colored glass bottles are the great defenders of a wine's virtue. Extensive research, serving both the beer and wine industries (beer also is susceptible to sunlight) reveals that brown bottles are significantly better than green bottles for wine storage; the darker the shade of brown, the better. This surely was welcome information to the wine producers of the Rheingau in Germany and the Piedmont in Italy, where dark brown bottles are traditional. Ideally, an opaque bottle would be used, but consumers prefer something a little more revealing, although some port bottles are as near opaque as one could wish.

What of artificial light? Will the rays from an incandescent or fluorescent bulb adversely affect one's wines in the same manner as sunlight? Ultraviolet radiation can affect a wine without heat being involved. The reaction is photochemical in nature. Here the research underscores the role of intensity in photochemical reactions in wine. Wines exposed constantly to fluorescent light, as in a wine shop, are thought to be subject to the harmful effects of ultraviolet and other wavelengths. But the degree of intensity falls too far short for any effect at all, with the possible exception of wines stored in a small cabinet with several fluorescent tubes going full blast nearly all day and night.

This caveat is due to research performed by the beer industry. Although beer appears more sensitive to the effects of light than wine, the results of tests on beer are not to be disregarded. Three Australian researchers reporting in the trade publication *Brewer's Digest* (1983) note that "while the intensity of [artificial] light is significantly less than that of direct sunlight, the overall spectrum of light from a fluorescent tube may very well match that of sunlight and, combined with long exposure times such as may occur in a display cabinet, the exposure to light may be equivalent to or greater than exposure to direct sunlight."

Using a standard commercial two-glass-door refrigerated display cabinet with two 40-watt fluorescent tubes for internal lighting and one 40-watt tube for back-lighting the display sign outside the cabinet, they discovered, using a triangular taste-testing procedure with a ten-member panel, that "formation of 'light-struck' flavor can occur in 750ml. [dark brown] bottles within two days in an illuminated cabinet." A standard wine bottle is 750 milliliters.

That said, it also was discovered that "beer stored on the bottom shelf, where the light intensity was not that great, was unaffected in all cases." This reveals just how critical the intensity factor is when considering the effects of artifical light. Even a matter of inches, as was the case in the close confines of the display cabinet, was enough to make an enormous difference. As fluorescent lights in groceries and wine shops are lofted high above any displays, the light intensity is far too slight to have any effect over a short period of time.

All of this underscores a simple fact: Unless the wine is extremely close to the artificial light source and exposed to it constantly, artificial light has no harmful effect on wine. In sum, only sunlight makes a difference, although a super-insulated cellar with a 100-watt incandescent bulb burning in it for hours could make a difference—but only from the heat it throws off.

WINE AND SHIPPING

Any discussion of the cellaring of wine surely merits a look at the vagaries of shipping the item. There is little sense in closeting a goodly amount of wine in the most perfect conditions one can achieve, only to realize belatedly that the wine was blemished to begin with.

The wine trade is perennially ripe with tales of badly

shipped or poorly warehoused wines. Some of these are doubt-less apocryphal, while others are depressingly true. The para-dox of wine as it is sold in this country is that the vast majority of wines drunk here leave the winery, foreign or domestic, in impressively fine condition, yet every wine lover has stumbled upon poorly stored bottles, oxidized to oblivion or otherwise marred, years taken from their lives that can not be restored.

Tracing the source of this disfigurement is difficult, if not impossible. There is no question whatever that imported wines stored in this country taste more mature than the same wines stored in their place of origin. The vast size of America makes this a problem even for native wine. California wines tasted in New York can sometimes seem more advanced there than in California; fragile Pinot Noirs from Oregon can occasionally crumble in Chicago. Is anyone in particular at fault?

To understand how the pristine condition of a wine can get waylaid by the time it reaches your cellar, it is necessary to gain at least an overview of how wines arrive in the shops. Since many fine wines arrive from France, Italy, Spain, and Germany, as well as through London, where wines are pur-chased at daily auctions, the example is best served by ex-amining the importation of European wines. The conditions endured by West Coast wines shipped East are no different, although transport is often less prolonged and there is no prob-lem about customs. Shipping and storage conditions are crit-ical for certain wines. The most susceptible to bruising or blemishing from oxidation caused by higher heat levels, at every point along the way, are red Burgundies or Pinot Noirs. I recall one instance in which I had tasted a range of one firm's lovely red Burgundies during a swing through Burgundy. The wines were then shipped by a major national importer and stored in the warehouse of an Oregon local wholesaler, whose storage conditions I know first-hand to be at least acceptable. Only a few months after I had tasted the wines at the source, the owner of the firm came to this country, bringing with him the firm's enologist/winemaker. A tasting of the wines was held in the distributor's warehouse and the winemaker and I retired to an undisturbed corner to evaluate the same wines we had analyzed so carefully back in Burgundy.

The results were dismaying. All of the wines were altered. Each shared an "overlay" of oxidation that blurred the underlying differences between vineyards or communes. It was clearly a matter of shipping, as the fault was the same for each wine, regardless of its price or status. The winemaker ruefully agreed. The wines were hardly ruined, but they were less than they should have been. And in this instance, both the national importer and the wholesaler were of sound reputation, except for the fact that in ideal circumstances such delicate wine would have been held in a temperature-controlled environment at every step of the way. The wines never did fully recover their original vibrant freshness of fruit.

Pinot Noir is an extreme instance, although many wines with low alcohol or pronounced fruitiness (German Rieslings, Loire whites, Beaujolais) are also susceptible to shipping distresses. This is not the same, it should be noted, as "bottle sickness." Many wines will frequently arrive bottle sick, out of sorts, but they will always recover. This is often revealed by a flat taste and is most commonly found immediately after bottling. The wine absorbs oxygen during the bottling process, resulting in a formation of acetaldehyde (a type of acidity) as well as a temporary loss of bouquet. It usually returns to health in one to three weeks. Champagnes, for instance, are prone to temporary bottle sickness, yet in fact they probably ship better than any other wine, the carbon dioxide of the bubbles helping to protect the wine.

Young wines always ship better than older bottles. Many buyers who intend to cellar wines for extended periods make a point of purchasing young wines, not only because the price is at its lowest and availability at its greatest, but also to preclude any possibility of poor storage of the wine in the ensuing years. Whatever the faults of their own cellars, they at least know what they are.

Older wines are by far the more likely to suffer. One

should be exceedingly cautious in purchasing older bottles of wine, older in this instance meaning anything ten years beyond the vintage date. Concern about provenance—the whereabouts of the wine prior to your purchase—is even more compelling if the wine is a red Burgundy or any white wine. How long has the merchant been in possession of the wine? If purchased recently (within the last year or two), where was the wine before that? Ideally, it may have lain untouched at the source and been imported directly. Or it may have been purchased at auction from a private cellar. Auction houses such as Christie's and Sotheby's in London are specific about informing prospective purchasers about the provenance of wines going under the gavel, at least when the provenance is noteworthy. Nowadays, though, too many wines shuttle back and forth across the Atlantic, only to wind up on the auction block where they first started out. Ultimately, you'll have to take the merchant's word for it, but it is important to ask. If nothing else, you put him on notice that you are not some credulous chump.

This is not to say that wine merchants are characteristically out to fleece or defraud the customer. Rather, many merchants have either little control over their storage space (by virtue of having none, the shop floor comprising the whole of it) or simply pay too little attention to it, accepting their storage conditions as inevitable. The cost of electricity is rising. For many merchants, the amount of business they do in older wines in negligible and they (sometimes mistakenly) trust to the resiliency of youth for their younger bottlings.

Big, strong wines such as young red Bordeaux, Cabernet Sauvignons, Nebbiolos, Merlots, Zinfandels, port, and the like are impressively resistant. And when affected, they are surprisingly resilient. Some white wines, such as Chardonnays, sweet whites such as Sauternes, Auslese-level or beyond Rieslings, sweet Chenin Blancs from the Loire, and Sauvignon Blancs are also quite sturdy. They are still more fragile, though, than reds, lacking the additional protection of the substantial tannins that young red wines can have. Pinot Noir, in my opinion, must be classed with the white wines as far as fragility is concerned. The more delicate the taste and structure of a wine, due to age or style, or where a fresh fruity quality is fundamental to its appeal, the more susceptible it will be to the wearying effects of shipping and the more concerned one should be about its shipping and storage conditions. No matter how tempting the price, there is no such thing as a good buy when the wine itself has already said *adieu*.

The overwhelming majority of European wines are sent to this country by ship, typically in twenty- or forty-foot-long containers. These sealed containers, which are a commonplace sight, are available to importers in three versions: a "dry," or, uninsulated, container; an insulated container; and a temperature-controlled, or "reefer," container, which is an insulated container in which the internal temperature-control system is operating. A twenty-foot container, the size frequently used by many importers, holds approximately seven hundred to one thousand cases of wine.

How this container is filled depends a great deal upon the size and sophistication of the importer. A major national importer such as Seagram Château & Estate Wines, which is owned by Joseph E. Seagram and Sons, Inc., imports such sizable quantities of wine that for, say, a shipment of Bordeaux, they need do little more than instruct the châteaux involved to expect a pickup (or to deliver) at a certain time and a container is "consolidated" in a matter of a few days. It would usually spend almost no time at dockside and be under way to the Port of New York from Le Havre, the most common point of departure for Bordeaux wines.

For a smaller shipper, or just for a more varied shipment, a freight forwarder or consolidator will assemble cases of wine sent to a central point from all over Europe—German wines, Burgundy, Bordeaux, Loire, Spanish, Italian, and so on. If everybody expedites his order as instructed, a container is assembled, the consolidator meets the ship's schedule, and the shipment is dispatched with little delay. Should one part of the order not arrive on time, the partially filled container may be sent out anyway, or it may be held on the docks or in a warehouse until the full order is assembled. Problems can easily arise in this situation.

The type of container employed can affect the condition of the wine in both the winter and summer months, when extremes of temperature are the most threatening. The best form of transport is the temperature-controlled container in which the temperature-control unit is active at all times, at the docks as well as in the hold of the ship. Such a container is an expensive proposition and very few importers, to the best of my knowledge, are so punctilious. They submit, sometimes justifiably so, that not only is the cost difference prohibitive for all but the most expensive wines, but that if wine shipments are avoided in midwinter and midsummer, such precautions are unnecessary.

Some importers use only insulated containers, contending that the vast majority of shipping situations require no more than that precaution. Yet others take what they can get, noting that insulated containers, which cost more than the so-called dry containers, hold about 25 percent less because of the bulk of the insulation, and the ribbed design of the interior of the container, which permits circulation of temperature-controlled air. But insulated containers can often be unavailable at certain ports (Spanish ones, for example) and are infrequently available at best. And the choice between a dry container and paying the premium for reserving a temperature-controlled one is considered so uneconomic as to be no choice at all.

Does any of this make a difference? Hard to say. Studies using recording thermometers were performed by Johnson ScanStar, a major shipper from Europe to West Coast ports, revealing that an uninsulated or dry container, shipped under the deck of the ship with an initial interior temperature of 50 degrees Fahrenheit, reached a high of 77 degrees at the Panama Canal during the month of April. It then recovered to almost exactly the same temperature as it began with upon arrival in Los Angeles. An insulated container on the same voyage reached a high of only 68 degrees at the Panama Canal point.

The opportunities for a lapse in optimal storage conditions occur at several points along this stage of the journey. The winery can usually be absolved of all possible fault; I have yet to visit a winery that was not punctilious about the storage conditions of its wines. What lapses might occur will likely be at dockside. The weather will have to be extreme, either well below freezing (wine freezes at about 27 degrees Fahrenheit) or extremely hot. And it must remain that way for several days. After all, the wine is protected by cardboard or wood boxes, both good insulators. Moreover, like a grove of trees where those on the perimeter take the brunt of inclement weather, a majority of the cases will be buried deep within a stack, which offers that much more insulating effect.

But lapses do occur and the most extreme examples, which seem to be rare, are dismaying. Often they involve extended holding of wines on the dock or even on the ship before being released to the importer. One instance occurred in New York City some years ago. The owners of a ship carrying a sizable quantity of First Growth red Bordeaux (Lafite, Mouton, Latour, Margaux, Haut-Brion) went bankrupt. The ship sat in the harbor in midwinter for two weeks, so the story goes, waiting for permission to offload. By the time the financial smoke cleared, the entire lot of wine had frozen. Yet you may be sure that there was no repeat of the Boston Tea Party using expensive First Growth Bordeaux.

A similar, even more prolonged, situation transpired in Portland, Oregon, involving delicate Asti Spumantes and German Rieslings. The owners couldn't pay, the customs office impounded the wine in its warehouse, and there it sweltered for several summers until the wines were finally sold at auction. Yet shortly thereafter, a local retailer (of no proven reputation) trumpeted the arrival of a bargain, name-brand Asti Spumante, along with a clutch of "wonderful" German white wines at too-good-to-be-true prices.

Although the possibility for freezing or overheating a

wine is always present during the importation phase, it is doubtful whether it is the source of most wine-storage woe, at least with respect to major or sophisticated shippers. Smaller merchants who are new to the game, or whose orders are consolidated with those of other small purchases to create a containerload (shipping lines charge by the type of item shipped and for space rather than by weight), may well engage, knowingly or inadvertently, in less rigorous shipping practices. Smart importers always specify that containers be stored "below deck and away from boilers, preferably forward." Otherwise, a container may be stored above deck, critically exposed to the elements. A trans-Atlantic journey takes eight to ten days to reach a major East Coast port; a voyage from Europe to the West Coast requires an average of twenty-five days.

A number of importers queried asserted that they tried not to engage in shipping during the summer months if at all possible; one importer averred that if they had to ship in the summer, they always employed a temperature-controlled container placed in the special temperature-controlled hold of the ship, a practice they normally did not employ at any other time of year. Nevertheless, wines frequently are shipped in July, because the entire process from placement of the order to arrival of the wine in the warehouse may take from 90 to 120 days. Wines meant to be sold in November must be shipped in July, because the French and other Europeans take a national holiday during the month of August. Orders only placed in July may not actually get shipped until September, if staff schedules and ship schedules fail to mesh, which is a fair likelihood. The wines may therefore arrive too late for Thanksgiving or even Christmas or will not at least have much time to recover from the usual "bottle sickness" brought about by shipping.

As for time spent on the docks, it is reasonable to conclude that well-established importers are unlikely to allow their merchandise to remain uncollected for long. Demurrage or dockside storage charges begin after five days at many ports and the fees are substantial. Also, most importers specialize in quick turnover. Wines are imported for immediate sale to distributors or to the public, rather than for inventory. The sooner off the dock, the better. An eight-hundred-case container, even though it is typically a combination of expensive and inexpensive wines, still represents an investment of anywhere from $50,000 to $100,000 a container. Very large importers might even have a container carrying as much as $1,000,000 worth of wine, although that is rare.

But when it gets to the warehouse, what then? Here we encounter a weaker link in the chain. Much depends upon the type of importer. Wines may arrive at one of three destinations: a national importer's distribution warehouse, to be forwarded by truck, rail, or even again by ship to a multitude of local distributors around the country. It may arrive directly to a local wholesaler who sells the wine to retailers. Or in some states the retailer himself may engage in what is called direct importing. The warehouse or cellaring conditions for each entity can and do vary dramatically, as does the length of stay in either a warehouse or on shop floor.

The national importer will usually warehouse wines for comparatively brief periods, although certain wines might remain for years before being absorbed by their network of local distributors. Much depends upon the pattern of buying by the importer and, of course, the nature of the market. Sometimes a major importer finds itself with excess stocks of famous and usually sought-after wines. A decision is made to hedge their losses (usually a matter of interest expenses) and sell the lot at a radically reduced price. So there are circumstances when too-good-to-be-true wine bargains can be found, but these are still unusual and are frequently the specialty of only the biggest markets. One Los Angeles merchant, Trader Joe's, is legendary for its offerings of fine wines at stupendously low prices.

Shipment from an importer's distribution warehouse to all parts of the country can pose some threat to the well-being of a wine, especially if the shipment occurs during the warmest or the coldest months or to exceedingly cold or hot cities. The New Orleans and Houston docks, points of arrival or departure for many wines, are famous for soaring summertime temperatures and pretty balmy circumstances even in winter. New York, Chicago, and Miami are also noted for temperature extremes that have been known to affect wine shipments. Wines shipped by rail or truck, especially when these are not temperature-controlled (which is typical), can sometimes be delayed or waylaid, often in extreme weather conditions. Again, it's not commonplace, but it does occur.

The weakest link is the storage of the wines by the local distributors and retailers. An extraordinary number of winemakers, wine brokers, and shippers have conceded in discussions on this topic that the great majority of wholesalers and retailers have conditions in their warehouses or store premises that range from inadvisable to deplorable. The usual problem is excessive heat during the summer months, especially in those states subject to prolonged, high summer temperatures. Wines stored near the roof of the structure (made possible due to steel racks) are particularly prone to heat damage. Sometimes, in a slow economy for example, a wholesaler or retailer may retain wines for several summers. The better wholesalers have at least adequate wine storage conditions. Some try to locate in old warehouses with deep stone or brick cellars that maintain a naturally cool condition. But these are rare, as well as inconvenient, as they usually are on several levels. Most new warehouses are constructed of sheet metal or tilt-up concrete slabs. Although these can be outfitted with temperature control devices, they rarely are.

Many wine distributors, especially in the Eastern and Sunbelt states, concentrate largely on hard liquor, the storage of which does not require the niceties of temperature control. Many warehouses that once held mostly liquor now can hold mostly wine, usually to the detriment of the wine. Overall, the generally poor conditions among wholesalers is improving, albeit slowly and reluctantly.

Retailers are the greatest offenders of all. Many keep their entire (and often slow-moving) stock on the floor of their establishment, which is necessarily heated in the winter—often overheated where steam heating is common—for human comfort. Few if any are allowed the luxury of the venerable London wine merchants like Berry Brothers and Rudd or H. Allen Smith, who display only a list of the wines available for sale. When you want a bottle or a case, a clerk is banished to the bowels of the cool cellar to fetch your order. It's a terrific system (for the wine), but doesn't make "marketing sense," as they say.

I cannot think of a single wine merchant in this country as punctilious as Jean-Claude Vrinat in Paris, who owns not only the three-star restaurant Taillevent, but a small retail wine shop as well. There he displays what appears to be the actual bottle of wine offered. In fact, the bottle is a facsimile, perfectly outfitted with the identical label and capsule, but filled with water tinted the appropriate color, rather than wine. All of the wines are stowed deep beneath the shop and are fetched upon command.

Most small wine retailers have no other storage facility than the shop floor itself. Even larger merchants, who do have storage facilities, are suspect. A surprising number are curiously reticent when asked about the temperature conditions of their storage areas. You would think that those who have installed temperature control mechanisms (or even a large air-conditioner) would trumpet the fact, but one hears little bugling.

Ideally, a serious and conscientious merchant would keep a recording thermometer in his or her cellar or warehouse and, after a year's time, display the results. One can hear the objections already: too much trouble; positively silly; our customers are fully satisfied already as to the condition of the wines we sell; we stand behind our wines. Harrrumph. Nevertheless, even though it should be apparent at this point that the retailer may himself be the recipient of blemished wines, she or he usually is the sole point of contact with the customer. And the sooner and more effectively he can exculpate himself

144 · *Making Sense of Wine*

from any blame for blemishing a wine through poor storage conditions, the better for all concerned. Pointing to the customer's ongoing satisfaction, one regrets to say, is too often pointing out most people's ignorance in the matter rather than a confirmation of the knowledgeability of the clientele.

7. The Presentation of Wine

Glasses are placed in a semi-circle either in front of the plate or else on the right; arrange these according to the courses to be served. First, water glass; second, white wine; third, sherry; fourth, Rhine wine; fifth, champagne; and sixth, Bordeaux. . . . Glasses intended for dessert wines and liquors, are only put on the table with dessert.

—Charles Ranhofer
The Epicurean (1893)

I once worked as a consultant to a major retailer of crystal. I was hired to advise the staff on which of the hundreds of glasses they sold would be best for wine and why. To do this right I had to see their side of things. So I worked the floor to gain a better understanding of what customers were asking. I got far more of an education than I gave.

The lesson learned, the one point that became increasingly clear, involved choosing the "correct" glass. Without fail, a prospective customer would beseech me to reassure him or her that the glass under consideration would be correct. This was paramount, and the fear of a social gaffe palpable. I am not ashamed to say that every time, without regard to how hideous the glass or inappropriate the design, I told them that it was just fine. "Of course," I would add, "you might find that your Champagne will keep its bubbles much longer if you serve it in this tall narrow glass rather than the coupe you are considering." Sometimes I could gently steer them to a more appropriate design, but the effort was not so much one of educating the client to the needs of the wine as of girding their social loins to stand up, psychologically anyway, to the anticipated raised eyebrows of their friends. The imagined and dreaded comment of their friends when presented with what is, in fact, an ideal Champagne glass was: "Isn't this an odd glass to serve Champagne in?" The host then has to bluff his or her way through the genteel challenge by displaying superior knowledge of Champagne and its needs. That takes guts, especially if you aren't previously recognized as knowing something about wine.

Prior to the Industrial Revolution, which began in England in about 1760 but really took off in the 1800s, there was no such thing as the wrong wineglass because using many different-shaped glasses at one sitting was almost unknown. But by the 1700s, the set of matched glasses of one, or at most, two, shapes on a table was a social necessity among the upper classes. This came about because the same English revolution that gave rise to the inexpensive glass bottle for wine in the mid-1600s—the addition of lead to the silica mixture for strength and clarity—also affected wineglasses. According to David Revere McFadden, curator of decorative arts for the Cooper-Hewitt Musum in New York, by 1667 the famed Ravenscroft factory already offered an array of glasses for "Clarrett, Sacke [a sweet, fortified wine, usually sherry] and Brandy." The capacity of the glass, rather than a wine-enhancing distinction of shape, differentiated one glass from another. The claret (red Bordeaux) glass held five ounces while the brandy glass held two ounces.

The dilemma of the correct glass dates to the mid-1800s, first in England and later elsewhere. The origins are clear: Wealth created by the Industrial Revolution was so vast that it greatly expanded the middle class. For the first time ever in Western civilization, a sizable group of people had enough money to look beyond their immediate needs of food, shelter, and clothing. The niceties were in reach at last. Eager to establish themselves in the new social order, they took their cues from their perceived betters, the landed gentry, and became acutely conscious of proper manners and forms of behavior, including how to set a table. Having a set of glasses already was established as the thing to do.

It was only when wealth became competitive and urban, when its display took forms other than land or livestock, that a new desire for more display at table emerged. Daily meals became longer and more involved, as well as much more highly structured. In the 1850s the mode of grand dinners changed from the *service à l'anglaise*, or English service, in which everything is presented at one time as in a buffet, to the *service à la russe*, or Russian, in which courses are brought by waiters to the table one course at a time.

Not only did this lengthen the time spent at table, but it demanded an orchestration of foods and wines on the part of the host. Previously, red and white wines were set out together, consumed as higgledy-piggledy as the food. With *service à la russe*, the free-for-all was over and with it, individual choice, the decision having already been made by the host. Not only did this call for a degree of astuteness about food and wine on the part of the host never before required, it also called for different glasses to reflect the new delicacy of distinctions being drawn. The desire for display was gratifyingly served as well.

The abundance of books on etiquette published between 1840 and 1910, to say nothing of afterward, is evidence of the need felt and the numbers who felt it. This insecurity could be answered only by a codification of rules. With rules you are safe, as all you need do is learn them and stay within their boundaries. It might also be noted in passing that this fit perfectly with a newly evolving social order: Etiquette is a way of keeping everyone in his place and of distinguishing who is out of place by virtue of his not knowing how to behave.

From this arose the specter of the correct wineglass. As Charles Ranhofer's precise instructions reveal, each type of wine was to have its own glass. The problem was in making sure that the shape of each glass was distinctively different from the others, never mind whether it served the need of the wine to its best advantage. The result was the exclusive use of the coupe, a shallow, wide-mouthed glass, for Champagne, which does nothing for Champagne except exhaust its bubbles faster than any other design. On the other hand it signaled, as it does to this day, the intent to serve Champagne. Or the port glass, which is little more than a large thimble invariably filled to the rim—a necessity given its size—that guarantees the drinker no opportunity for savoring the perfume of a good port. The largest glass was always reserved for water. It still is, which is a waste because the red wines that really need the extra room are instead confined to smaller quarters. All of these glasses are in common and accepted use today; indeed, they are considered "correct."

Is there such a thing as a correct glass? And how important is it? It's bad form to answer a question with a question, but I'll do it anyway: How important is the wine to you? If the wine matters little, then, no, there's no such thing as the correct glass. You should choose what pleases your eye and give no further thought to the matter. This offhand approach to wine has been in effect for centuries and it didn't seem to prevent our ancestors from identifying the finest wines, so it can't be all bad.

But if you're reading this book, it's a good guess that wine means something to you, in which case, appropriate glasses are essential. Please note the key word *appropriate*. The term *correct* smacks of etiquette, rather than sensibility. Various glasses can be appropriate for the same type of wine without in the least resembling each other, at least superficially. For instance, in Burgundy the glass of choice among the growers, for both red and white Burgundies, is a brandy snifter. This makes sense, as Burgundies are about perfume above all else and the funnel shape of the snifter is the ideal vehicle for exploiting this quality. Other, less exaggerated, shapes can achieve the same end.

On the other hand, you can't always look to growers to do right by their wines when it comes to presenting them in a glass that shows them off. One of the most extreme examples of this confronted me at, ironically, one of the most memorable wine tastings I've ever been privileged to experience. I was visiting the Mosel-Saar-Ruwer district and, through the courtesy of an acquaintance, wangled a private tasting at the estate of Egon Müller. Müller's wine is the famed Scharzhofberger, a Riesling from the sixty-seven-acre Scharzhofberg vineyard in the Saar, of which Müller owns one-quarter, and the best part at that. It is considered one of Germany's greatest vineyards and Müller is its acknowledged master.

The Müller style for tastings is to present the wines in a circle of glasses placed on a small round table in the foyer of the old manor house that sits at the foot of the vine-encrusted hill that is the Scharzhofberg. The wines laid out before me were wondrous: an array of 1983 Scharzhofbergers including such rarities, produced in minute quantities, as Beerenausleses and Eisweins. Older vintages dating back to the early seventies also were served, all from newly opened bottles. I couldn't help but wonder what they did for somebody important! But there was a hitch. All of these wondrous wines were served in tiny glasses, each holding perhaps three ounces—but only when filled to the brim, which they were. It was impossible to give the wines their due, as the glass offered no room for the delicate fragrance of the Scharzhofbergers to collect. It was not a matter of frugality. Every wine came from a freshly opened bottle which was placed behind each glass, so as to allow replenishing if desired.

Dismayed as I was, I can't say that I was completely surprised, although I did expect that a grower of such painfully high standards as Müller—he really is in a class by himself— would have extended those standards to how he presents his wines. German wine typically is served in Germany in a "hock" glass (a British term coined in the Victorian era after the village and wine of Hochheim), which is a small cup mounted on a long, thin, often green-colored stem. Sometimes the cup, rather than the stem, is green, an old device used to hide the cloudiness of long-ago wines. The cup always is filled to the top. The notion is that Rieslings are so fragrant that the scent spurts from the glass. Granted, they are as user-friendly as a Labrador retriever and as enjoyable, but no wine of quality is the better for such treatment.

The relationship between a fine wine and its glass has long been overlooked, taken for granted, or even sneered at by a surprising number of otherwise wine-knowledgeable people. It seems pretentious, even for wine, which seems capable of supporting quite a burden of pretension as it is. It can seem overly fussy. It isn't. No one would dispute that Château Lafite-Rothschild would taste substantially different if drunk out of cupped hands as opposed to a well-designed wine glass. Actually, cupped hands are not as poor a vehicle, drips aside, as some wineglasses. The warmth of your hands warms the wine nicely, urging it to release its bouquet. The tight enclosure of two hands cupped closely acts as a funnel for the fragrance, and in order to drink from your hands you have to stick your nose pretty deeply into the make-do vessel, with the benefit of a good rich sniff before drinking. Even the act of drinking benefits, as you have to slurp it up, which oxygenates the wine and further volatilizes the numerous components of its smell. This is why professional wine tasters are always seen—and heard—practically gargling wines before either swallowing or spitting.

Still, cupped hands are not as effective as a well-designed glass and not just for reasons of practicality or dry-cleaning costs. Different wines need different amounts of space. Apart from the aesthetics and quality of the glass, two design features are critical: the size of the cup and its shape. Different wines need different-size cups. Some, such as red Burgundies, blossom only when a proportionately small amount of wine is contained in a generous, semienclosed space so as to allow the delicate but abundant perfume of the wine to collect. Others, such as Muscat or Riesling, are less in need of space for their penetrating scent to collect. Here the amount of wine is the source of the charge, rather than airspace for elusive fragrances to be collated and contained. This is why the German hock glass, ineffective as it is, still is plausible: There's always plenty of wine in the cup. What it needs is a little more airspace.

Is there such a thing as the perfect, all-purpose glass? Various designs have been submitted as such, with varying results of effectiveness. In general, the best wineglasses hold a generous amount of wine in a clear, plain cup, with no engraving or cutting, that curves inward to collect and contain the "nose" or scent of the wine. For what it's worth, I'm pleased with my own choice, which has served successfully for virtually every sort of wine except Champagne. I use it in my wine-tasting classes, so it has seen service for thousands of different wines over the years. And I've also compared its performance to what I consider reference-standard wineglasses from Riedel and Baccarat, about which more in a moment.

The design of the glass usually is referred to as a chimney shape: The cup is slightly bulbous at the base and then tapers cleanly and gracefully to a smaller opening at the top, which creates a funnel effect. The reason I am so fond of this particular version is that the proportions are just right. The glass is 7 inches in height, which makes it easy to hold and not overpoweringly large or heavy in the hand. It holds fourteen ounces when filled to the brim, which of course is not the idea. Instead, a good serving is three to four ounces, or only one-quarter full, which leaves plenty of airspace for the fragrance to collect. The tapering shape contains it and also prevents the wine from sloshing out if you swirl it. It's amazing how much wine can fly out of some glasses when swirled.

The only wine that does not do well in the chimney glass is sparkling wine. This is because of the peculiar needs of wines with bubbles, namely that bubbles like to find a point from which to lodge and then drift upward. Because of this, good Champagne glasses share several common elements: The base of the cup tapers to a sharp point to create a takeoff point for the bubbles; the shape is narrow rather than broad, so as not to provide too much surface area from which the carbon dioxide bubbles can dissipate; and the cup tapers inward at the top. The ideal sparkling-wine glass is known as a tulip shape, as its inward-curving sides mimic the shape of the flower.

Sparkling wines are exceptionally sensitive to the cleanliness of the glass, as the bubbles will fail to form in a glass containing the slightest trace of a greasy film, dust, or detergent. A wet glass is deadly to the bubbles. The film prevents the bubbles from forming in the same soothing way as the proverbial oil poured on troubled waters. In this case, however, we're looking for trouble. The bubbles form as a result of friction between the carbon dioxide trapped in the wine and the roughness of the glass. This explains why sparkling wines served in crystal, which has a lead content of 24 percent to 30 percent in its mix, display more bubbles than when served in noncrystal glasses composed of silica mixed with either potash or soda alkali. Crystal is microscopically rougher than glass, resulting in more friction between wine and wine glass.

I once had no end of difficulty with my Champagne glasses, despite the fact that they were stored in an enclosed cupboard hanging upside down from a rack, like bats, to drip dry. Despite the fact that I rinsed them assiduously, a few glasses out of the seventy-five or so used in the course of a wine-tasting class managed to suppress the bubbles. The bubbles would miraculously emerge when the wine was poured from the offending glass into a new, apparently cleaner one. But I couldn't figure out where I had gone wrong.

I got the answer not from a winery, but from the brewmaster of a local brewery. Even more than sparkling wine producers, breweries are tremendously concerned about the cleanliness of the glasses in which their beers are served. A filmy, wet, or dusty beer glass will flatten a beer like a flyswatter. I told my lament to the brewmaster, who then inquired what detergent I was using. At the time I was still laboriously washing the glasses by hand—I now have the luxury of a special commercial glass-washer that washes thirty-six glasses in a four-minute cycle—and I reported that I was using a standard liquid dishwashing detergent. But, I added defensively, I was rinsing the glasses scrupulously in hot water. He said that the detergent was the problem: They contain various fats or glycerine, which help make and hold suds. These fats cling to the glass and unless the rinsing is performed almost fanatically with very hot water, likely will remain on the glass. The answer, I learned, was to use electric dishwasher detergent instead, even when washing by hand. You just get few suds, but the glasses are still clean. Since that revelation, I have had no further difficulties with Champagne glasses unless they go too long between cleanings, when they pick up grease and dust from the air.

As for particular Champagne glasses, I use two: a cheap and an expensive. The cheap one is an especially well made Champagne tulip of perfect proportions from a company called Riekes Crisa. Unlike most of the inexpensive Champagne tulips on the market, which have an unsightly blob of glass where the stem attaches to the foot, the Riekes version is handsomely sculpted and holds eight ounces, which is a good size. The glass is called an eight-ounce Tulip Champagne #2254. Riekes Crisa is owned by the Alco Standard Company, 1818 Leavenworth St., Omaha, Nebraska 68102. It costs about $8 a tulip, depending upon the seller.

The expensive glass is a distinctive beauty that you now see in all sorts of atmospheric advertisements—and many French Champagne ads—from Baccarat. The pattern is called Dom Perignon and, *quelle horreur*, it is not a classic tulip. Instead, the Dom Perignon design—which first appeared in 1961—is a V-shape, flaring ever so slightly from a base with a point so sharp it looks like it was shaped by a pencil sharpener. Champagnes taste and smell great in it, and although I'm not about to suggest that it is superior to the tulip shape, I will say that it is almost as good. It feels wonderful in your hand and next to your lip. The price, however, doesn't feel so good: about $55 a glass. The other good design from Baccarat, in the classic tulip shape, is their St. Remy pattern, which is admirable.

Like so many Baccarat designs, the company offers the Dom Perignon style in a gradation of styles labeled red wine, white wine, water glass, and Champagne flûte. Ironically, the Champagne flûte is not what I would recommend. Like all flûtes, it is very narrow. The problem is that it holds too little wine, the narrowness makes the wine froth excessively when first poured, and, worst of all, it's so narrow that it is hard to drink from it. The glass of choice for Champagne actually is the red-wine version. It's lousy for red wine—it flares out rather than in—but this is less of a concern for champagne, which powers its scent to you through the turbocharging of the bubbles. The red-wine Dom Perignon holds just the right amount: seven ounces.

While on the subject of Baccarat, I may as well bring up my other choice for an all-purpose wineglass, albeit an expensive one. It is the Baccarat pattern called Haut-Brion. (They like to name their wineglasses after famous French vineyards, although the owners gallingly get nothing in exchange.) The Haut-Brion style is one of Baccarat's greatest design achievements and, sad to say, one of their marketing failures. At their best, Baccarat designers have a gift for how a glass, filled, feels in the hand; in making the foot of the glass heavy enough to provide just the right counterbalance; in getting the proportions just so. There's nothing unusual or outlandish in the Haut-Brion design. It's essentially an elongated egg-shape in which the top third has been sheared off. It is 7 inches tall and holds twelve ounces when completely filled. Many other glassmakers have issued a similar glass. But the refinements of balance and heft, that indefinable feel as in custom-made jewelry, sets this apart as the standard against which other versions are measured.

So what's the problem? The problem is that Baccarat decided to discontinue making the Haut-Brion line because it didn't sell—except for just one size glass in the lineup. Happily, the one glass saved from extinction is the best one in that design, an excellent size for both red and white wines. I've yet to taste a wine, red or white, that didn't show exceptionally well in this glass with its inward-curving sides.

I hesitate to rave over this glass, yet have no choice because it is so perfect, because Baccarat, Inc., the official name for the American distribution branch, refuses to bring in the glass, citing a lack of interest. This unwillingness is odd, if only because the French mother company owns the American branch outright, so all that's going on is a matter of money and goods going from the corporate left hand to the right hand. No less a figure than the director-general of Baccarat in France, Yves du Petit Thouars, in a recent interview about wine-glasses, pointed out the Haut-Brion glass, calling it "really wonderful." And so it is.

The answer is to send for it directly from France, which hardly is convenient, but is not that forbidding either. Any Baccarat dealer in France can obtain it. I can recommend three such places, having visited two and ordered through a third: the Baccarat company's own retail shop in the town of Baccarat (Magasin de Vente au détail de la Compagnie des Cristailleries de Baccarat, rue des Cristailleries, 54120 Baccarat, France, Tel. 83.75.12.47); another crystal retailer in Baccarat, a town that has crystal shops like Las Vegas has casinos (Vessière Cristaux, 54120 Baccarat, France, Tel. 83.75.10.55); and a Baccarat dealer in Cannes, which is noteworthy because it keeps an enormous inventory (Pavillon Christofle, 109 rue d'Antibes, 06400 Cannes, France, Tel. 93.38.54.06). All three have staff that speak English and all accept major credit cards. To telephone from the States you first have to dial the international access code, 011, and then the country code for France, which is 33. Then you dial the number.

A third Baccarat glass, also a commonly seen shape but, like the Haut-Brion, inimitable in feel and balance, is the spherical Bourgogne or Burgundy glass. Looking like a perfect sphere with only the topmost section removed, the idea of such a glass is to allow the scent of the wine to collect in a

large, enclosed space. No red wines more reward such treatment than red Burgundies, hence the name. This glass is
available in the States. Since it comes in three sizes, one of
them improbably large and heavy, it is well to make sure that
you're getting the ideal version: It is 7½ inches high and holds
twenty ounces when completely full. When I ordered mine
from France, they had the following designation from Baccarat: Verre Degustation [tasting glass] 15879 UNI, which
presumably is the Baccarat code number.

Good as these Baccarat glasses are, the laurels for the
finest wineglasses available go to the Austrian crystal company
Riedel (pronounced REE-dle). The glasses are known as the
Sommeliers series, nearly all of them designed in the 1950s
by the late Claus Joseph Riedel, who discovered during a
dinner party when he ran out of one set of glasses and had to
substitute another design that the same wine tasted different
in the new glass. Design, he concluded, can affect actual taste.
He subsequently queried various authorities in anatomy,
physics, and enology to discover why this was so and then
proceeded to create glasses designed for specific categories of
wines: Champagne, Burgundy, old Bordeaux and young Bordeaux, Riesling, Sherry, and Chablis or Chardonnay.

Although it has long since been acknowledged that the
shape of a glass profoundly influences the amount and intensity
of the scent of a wine, the Riedel family goes one step further:
They believe that the shape of the glass influences the actual
taste of the wine—bitter, salty, sweet, and sour—as distinct
from smell. According to Georg Riedel, son of Claus Joseph,
in the English wine magazine *Decanter* (January 1988), "Nobody thinks about the act of drinking. It's a subconscious act.
We are aware of what signal our taste buds give, but nobody
considered when designing glasses that our taste buds are located in different parts of the tongue. The 'sweet' taste buds
are located on the tongue tip, so if you have a wine high in
acidity you will try to bring the wine to the tip of the tongue
to bring out its fruit and sweetness. You will not try to bring
the wine further into the mouth where the 'acidity' and 'salty'
taste buds are situated."

Georg Riedel avers that "a cylindrical shape, a glass with straight, parallel sides, is not good for wine: It takes out all the character. The narrower it is, the sweeter the taste; the wider, the more bitter and sour. It's simply the result of the way the wine flows from the glass into your mouth."

As to the veracity of these assertions I cannot say. But one thing is certain: Riedel Sommeliers series glasses are superb. At first I was a little put off by them, especially the Burgundy glass (Sommeliers series 400/16), which is far larger than what one normally considers a reasonable-size glass. Although only 9½ inches high, which is not that tall, its capacity is a whopping thirty-seven ounces, even though you still don't pour in more than three or four ounces of wine, as with any other glass. The shape is bulbous in the center, or paraison, to use the term glassmakers employ for identifying the widest point in a design, and is pinched inward at the rim with the slightest flaring to create a lip. The result is an enormous space in which the fragrance can collect, funneled through a smaller but still reasonably broad opening at the top.

When I first tried the Riedel Burgundy glass, its unfamiliar size seemed awkward and a little pretentious. A few uses later, it began to seem normal. Unlike every other outsized wineglass of my acquaintance, this one feels good in the hand, saved by an exquisite yet balanced lightness. (The Baccarat Burgundy glass weighs eight ounces empty; the Riedel Burgundy glass, with almost twice the capacity, weighs just ten ounces.) For what it's worth, this glass was chosen by the Museum of Modern Art in New York for its permanent collection in 1959, although for form rather than function.

Do red Burgundies taste better in it than in other glasses? As for actual taste, I'm not sure. But when it comes to appreciating the explosive scent of these wines, no other glass comes close. It's my first choice for both Burgundies and Barolos, although Riedel offers a separate Barolo glass that very closely resembles Baccarat's spherical Burgundy glass, in which Barolo certainly shows well.

The other Riedel Sommeliers designs are similarly inspired, especially the narrow Riesling glass (Sommeliers series

400/1), the tall, flûte-shaped Champagne glass (400/8), and the smaller Bordeaux glass (400/0), which holds twelve ounces compared to the larger version (400/00), which unlike the Burgundy glass is somehow clumsy and less rewarding to drink from. None of these glasses is cheap. They cost between $35 and $55 a glass. Riedel is available from a variety of retailers in the States, including Macy's department store in New York. One New York store that specializes in discounting name-brand crystal, including Riedel and Baccarat, is Robin Importers, Inc., 510 Madison Avenue, New York, New York 10022. In-state telephone is 212-752-5605; out-of-state is toll-free at 800-223-3373. When I last dealt with them they offered about 15 percent off the regular list price for both Riedel and Baccarat.

Something should be said about a group of glasses favored by some wine buffs, called Les Impitoyables, literally the pitiless or merciless in French. Designed by a French furniture and tablewear salesman, Jacques Pascot, this series of large crystal glasses is, like the Riedel Sommeliers series, designed to perform with certain categories of wines. Similarly large-scale, they can at least magnify various wines. But unlike the Riedel glasses, they are next to impossible to drink from due to the inappropriately small opening at the mouth, they are nowhere near as well balanced, and for some tasters—this one included—they seem to exaggerate rather than merely amplify without distortion. They reflect, sadly, the trend toward viewing wine as something to be studied apart from the table and as something akin to a laboratory specimen. They also are as expensive as Riedel and Baccarat.

In comparison to wineglasses, which are critical to our enjoyment of wine, the matter of decanters is simple in the extreme. There is no ideal shape nor, for that matter, is decanting a necessity. It only becomes so when a wine, invariably an older one, shows some sediment in the bottle. In order that no one receive murky wine as you get near the end of the bottle, the host decants the wine into a decanter and serves it from that rather than the bottle. The process, which somehow

It is true that certain very young, clean wines do seem more rewarding after, say, thirty minutes of exposure to air than just two or three minutes. This has more to do with the "tight-ness" of such young wines than any salutory benefit of aeration. The truth is that if a clean wine needs that much or more airing before being drinkable, you're drinking the wine too young. Mature wines are as forthcoming as experienced lovers. They need little encouragement.

I like decanting wines, whether sediment is present or not, simply for the beauty of a limpid wine in a sparkling clean decanter. And I like doing this for both red and white wines. It is easy to forget just how beautiful today's white wines are when they are seen only in small amounts in a rapidly draining wineglass. Also, there's the subtle psychological benefit of not seeing the wine label. I am not suggesting that wines should be served blind or with the label unseen. That is a silly, even vaguely sadistic practice that has no place at the table. Rather, it can sometimes be hard to forget that the wine you're drinking is the fabled Château Splendide or the rare, 1.2-acre Immaculate Conception Vineyard of Napa Valley, let alone what such wines cost. With the label constantly in view, the reminder, however innocent, exerts a force that may not always be welcome. A decanter removes this presence as elegantly as could be imagined. I like simply to present the bottle so that everyone knows what they are drinking and then remove the bottle from view altogether.

On a more mundane note, cleaning decanters, two problems sometimes present themselves: ridding the decanter of a red-wine haze and exorcising moisture from long-necked decanters that never quite seem to dry properly. The problem of decanters being stained by wine, invariably red, seems to be something that afflicts British drinkers more than American. The problem usually arises when a powerfully pigmented wine such as port is left for days, even weeks, in a decanter. This often happens in Great Britain, where during the winter months a decanter of port is always at the ready on a sideboard—a civilized habit. The problem is that when the decanter finally is empty and in need of cleaning, the wine has stained the interior and no amount of soap and water seems to do the trick. Here the microscopic roughness of crystal again has its effect, this time harboring pigments from wines.

Having had such problems myself, I can assert that the answer is easily at hand, although you wouldn't know it from the number of letters to British wine magazines pleading for a solution to the problem. You would think it an intractable problem to judge from the variety of answers to the dilemma, ranging from baking soda to using lead shot to the use of effervescent denture-cleaning tablets. (That one ought to work.) One of the perennial suggestions in British publications is the employment of finely crunched fresh eggshells placed in a stained decanter with a few tablespoons of water. One is supposed to shake this all around and then leave it to stand for several hours. I cannot attest to its efficacy.

But I can attest to simply using bleach. Just pour some in, without dilution, and carefully swirl it around the interior of the decanter. If the stain is not severe, the bleach magically removes it in an instant. If it is embedded, let it sit for an hour or so. No stain is the match for bleach. Then just drain the bleach and very thoroughly rinse multiple times with hot water. After four or five rinses all trace of the bleach and its smell will have disappeared and the decanter will sparkle.

As for the exasperating problem of drying the interior of long-necked decanters, which for reasons of poor interior air circulation always seem to retain some condensation, a solution is available. The answer is found in any chemical supply house in the form of crystals of calcium sulfate. You want to ask for the "indicating" version. A common brand name for indicating calcium sulfate is Dry-Rite. This substance absorbs moisture. It sells for about $10 a pound. You sometimes find small packets of it with camera equipment or other goods when the manufacturer doesn't want any moisture to enter the article. The indicating variety refers to the convenient feature of its changing color, usually to blue, when it has absorbed as much moisture as it can hold. Then all you do is place it in a 200-

degree oven to dry out. The color reverts to its original white and it's ready for reuse.

To use this substance for drying out decanters you will need to fashion a long "snake" of semiporous fabric that can easily be inserted through the neck of the decanter and will reach to the bottom and extend from the top for easy removal. The calcium sulfate should fill the tube and be permanently sewn in. Once your decanter is drained as well as possible, slip the tube inside and walk away. In a few hours or overnight, the remaining moisture will have been completely absorbed.

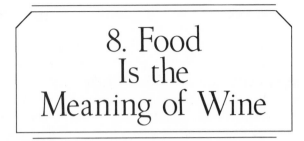

8. Food Is the Meaning of Wine

It is generally admitted by real gourmets that red wines should precede the introduction of white wines.

—Charles Elmé Francatelli
The Cook's Guide (1862)

The general mode of thinking always leans on the cliché and on the abstract. People do not return to their palates. People are afraid that they do not know how to taste. They prefer to lean on rules. With rules you don't have to think; you don't have to taste. You just have to follow the rules—and they'll destroy you every time.

—Richard Olney (1986 interview)
The Wine Spectator

Wines exist for food. Without the context of food, wine is a eunuch, a sterile experience that soon acquires distorted features. One instance of this was some of the California wines produced in the 1970s. The Zinfandels kept getting bigger and more alcoholic. The Cabernets grew more tannic and "flabby" from lack of acidity due to overripeness. The wines were made, tasted, and discussed in an atmosphere as removed from the table as a greenhouse is from the natural world, with similarly unreal results. Happily, winemakers and wine buyers alike came to their (gustatory) senses in the eighties and the wines are better than ever, not because of technology but of attitude. The environment of wine began to alter from that of the laboratory to that of the table. The changed quality of the experience was akin to that of seeing an animal in its native haunt rather than the artificiality of a zoo.

This context of food is essential. It is not coincidental that the two sources of the world's finest wines, France and Italy, also boast the finest cuisines in Europe. One can only wonder what the Chinese would have done with wine. Nor is it coincidental that in the New World, the increase in the quality of wines has paralleled almost lockstep the rise of interest in food and in better restaurants.

Where wine is viewed as a correspondent to food we find the following, regardless of the grape variety or culture: a liking for restraint over excess; a preference for higher acidity; an increasing desire for greater variety in tastes to better accommodate an increasing array of dishes; and not least, a certain insouciance about wine. The more it finds itself on the table, the less exacting one gets in trying to ensure that just the right wine goes with just the right dish. This flies in the face of the conventional portrait of the gourmet, who fusses over whether one vineyard or vintage is more ideal than another for a certain dish. It gets done, surely, but usually by those for whom wine with food is a special occasion, like hosts who use their best china and crystal on special occasions rather than throughout the year. Ludwig Bemelmans, that past master of the art of enjoying life, captured the tortured quality of the so-called gourmet. "Actually, the true gourmet, like the true artist, is one of the unhappiest creatures existent. His trouble comes from so seldom finding what he constantly seeks: perfection." Bemelmans exempted himself from this role. "As for being a gourmet, I disqualify in every respect. I eat too much, drink too much and love company at the table. I use the menu without attention to the rules."

The challenge today is that never before have so many different cuisines mingled with so many different wines, with nary a rule in sight. Not since the formalization of service and menus in the mid-1800s, where the incoherence of the *service à l'anglaise* was replaced with the orderliness of the *service à la russe*, has a host been confronted with so many choices and so little tradition upon which to comfortably lean.

Moreover, tastes have changed dramatically. A glance at menus of the late 1800s, no matter what the country, reveals a choice and progression of wines that is mystifying to the modern palate. A famous example is serving Sauternes, the rich, sweet wine of the eponymous district in Bordeaux, with raw oysters. Yet not only was it common practice in all the grand menus of Victorian Europe, but formulaic. Chablis also was served, it should be noted.

As Francatelli—who was head chef to Queen Victoria— points out, no host with pretensions to gourmandise in his time would dream of serving white wines before red. Yet today, serving reds before whites would be considered un- thinkable, as contemporary thinking has it that the greater intensity of flavor found in modern red wines will overwhelm the delicacy of the whites. This concern seemed absent a cen- tury ago: It was once common practice to serve Champagne with the beef course, to offer just one example of how far the wheel of taste has turned.

A good example is found in a dinner for fourteen people given by a Mr. Benson in Delmonico's restaurant in New York in 1883, reflecting a taste common on both sides of the At- lantic. The menu, which counted no less than twenty-nine dishes, included these pairings in this order:

Oysters—with Johannisberg [German Riesling, most probably sweet]

Clam bisque—with Madeira

Grilled lobster; Timbales of sheepshead with sauce Ambassadrice [a type of porgy or drum fish molded and sauced with a chicken stock and cream sauce, into which a chicken purée and whipped cream are blended]; and a *Tomato salad*— with Château d'Yquem

Vol au vents [puff pastry] filled with lamb's testicles in a finan- cière sauce; Terrapin with sauce Newberg—with Lachryma

Christi (Tears of Christ), then a rich, sweet wine, likely white but possibly red, from southern Italy. At the time it was one of the most extravagantly praised wines, a good example of this being a Dutch wine lover's lament—"Oh Christ, why didst thou not weep in my country?"

Beef fillet; Potato croquettes; Chicken casserole; Quenelles [dumplings] of squab with Jerusalem artichokes—with Château Larose, most likely the St. Julien Second Growth Château Gruaud-Larose, a red Bordeaux

Lamb Chops with a brown sauce—with Pommery Champagne

Asparagus with oil and a white wine sauce with horseradish and shallots—with Perrier-Jouët Champagne

Mushrooms on toast; Cheese soufflé; Sherbet—with sparkling Burgundy, most likely made from Pinot Noir grapes but pale or even white in color

Roasted English pheasant; Grilled ham; Fried bananas; Artichokes sauced with a crayfish-infused Hollandaise; and various desserts—with Clos Vougeot, the grand *cru* red Burgundy

Two features about this representative menu leap out, apart from its sheer excess: how richly sauced the dishes are and how chaotic their progression. It reveals one of those historical truths that hindsight often overlooks, namely, that the boundaries between the old and the new are no more sharp than between neighboring countries. Here the hodgepodge of the old *service anglaise* still makes itself felt in this *service russe* menu. It would take another twenty years and the influential genius of Escoffier to refine the menu into some kind of orchestration of tastes.

On the other hand, the choice of wines makes more sense than not. With the possible exception of Champagne with lamb chops, everything else is reasonable, given the richness of the saucing. In this, they had an insight that somehow has been lost: Rich goes with rich. A fish course presented with a cream reduction sauce infused with wine is better served by a sweet wine of high underlying acidity than by most dry white wines. Such wines—German Rieslings of the Spatlese and Auslese class; Sauternes; Vouvray *moelleux*; Quarts de Chaumes; Bonnezeaux; Lachryma Christi—are better thought of as rich rather than sweet, because when mature, the sweetness is subsumed by the fruit, and the once-jarring elements of sweetness, fruitiness, and acidity meld into a seamless whole. The resulting wine tastes rich, not sweet. When tasted with equally rich foods, it comes off as ideal and not at all sweet. In fact, the thought never even crosses your mind.

A good example of this is an exceptional dish that is easy to prepare, undeniably rich, and a perfect vehicle for exploring this business of rich with rich. The dish is an unusual combination of half a ripe avocado that has been poached to warm it through, served with an *oeuf mollet* or six-minute egg placed in the depression where the pit used to be and napped in a *sauce Béarnaise*.

WARM AVOCADO WITH OEUF MOLLET, SAUCE BÉARNAISE

TO SERVE FOUR PEOPLE: Ripen 2 avocados in a closed brown paper bag for several days until the avocado gives under gentle pressure. Bring a large saucepan of water to the boil. Prick holes at the large ends of 4 eggs and set aside. Slice the avocados lengthwise and peel the halves. Remove the pits. Using a large skimmer, lower the eggs and the avocado halves gently into the boiling water and immediately lower the heat to a very gentle simmer. Set the timer for 6 minutes. After 6 minutes remove the eggs to a large bowl of cold water to prevent further cooking. The yolk will be liquid while the white is firm. Remove the pan from heat, but let the avocado halves remain in the water to keep warm.

While the eggs and avocados are cooking (technically the avocados are not cooking, as they do not undergo change from the heat), prepare the Béarnaise sauce: In a heavy-bottomed saucepan combine 4 tablespoons of dry white wine, 4 tablespoons white wine vinegar, 1 tablespoon finely chopped shallots, 1 teaspoon dried tarragon *or* 1 tablespoon finely chopped fresh tarragon, and salt and white pepper to taste. Bring this to a boil and let it boil, uncovered, until it is reduced by two-thirds. Remove from heat and let cool completely. Melt 1½ sticks (6 ounces) unsalted butter and set aside momentarily.

Strain the herb reduction into a clean saucepan and place over very low heat. Add 2 egg yolks and whisk them into the vinegar reduction until it thickens noticeably. Then slowly dribble in the still-warm melted butter, whisking constantly. The sauce will thicken and mount. Check for taste and add more salt, white pepper or, even a sprinkle of finely chopped tarragon to taste.

TO SERVE: Remove the avocados from the water and blot dry with paper towels. Place one half each on warm, individual serving plates. Peel the eggs and put one whole egg in each avocado half. Spoon the Béarnaise sauce over the egg and avocado and serve immediately.

Here the rich with rich approach comes into its own. White wine is called for, but experience reveals that a surprising number of possibilities exist. The most obvious one —and no less good for being so—is a grand Chardonnay. The ideal choice is something on the order of a mature Corton-Charlemagne, which offers not only an invigorating stoniness, but an unctuosity as well. For this reason any of a number of the big, buttery California or Australian Chardonnays are worthy partners.

An even better choice, perhaps for its being unexpected, is a mature German Riesling. One of the best pairings, chosen on a lucky whim, was a Scharzhofberger Spatlese 1971 from Egon Müller, which proved equally inspiring. It also turns out that any of a number of Rheingaus work, as do mature Vouvray *moelleux* and Sauternes. All have the requisite texture. None taste the least bit sweet.

While on the topic of rich wines, they come into their own with an ingredient with which they are too rarely paired: smoked salmon. The traditional accompaniment of smoked salmon, at least if the budget lends itself to it, is Champagne. It goes well enough, although the appeal is largely a psychological one of luxurious with luxurious.

But the idea in choosing wines with certain foods is to come up with a combination in which each enhances the other. This is the famous marriage, which explains why it is so difficult. Smoked salmon is salty as well as oily, and the palate fatigues quickly. Champagne seems to refresh because of the bubbles, but it doesn't work. What's needed is a wine with some sweetness, which cancels out the saltiness. One of the best choices is a mature German Riesling from the Mosel/Saar/Ruwer. The most enjoyable combination yet tried has been a Maximin Grunhaus "Herrenberg" Auslese 1976, which gave the salmon a whole new dimension and vice versa. Recioto Soaves can be impressive, as can any rich wine with a high underlying acidity and not too overpowering a flavor. Sauternes doesn't work here, largely because of the assertiveness of the botrytis, or noble rot flavor. On the other hand, the classic combination of Sauternes with Roquefort cheese—which is terrifically salty and very assertive in flavor—*does* work. I still recall trying it for the first time on a trip through Southwest France, more than a little skeptical about the combination. It was a revelation.

What also works well with salmon, both fresh and smoked, is one of the most unappreciated white wines: Pinot Gris. The best versions come from Alsace, although Oregon is fast coming on with some good bottlings, as is northern Italy. Germany has long produced rich versions of Pinot Gris; it's known as Ruländer. At is best, Pinot Gris has a creamy texture that gives it an impression of richness while remaining bone dry, the German versions excepted. It also ages beautifully. In fact, the oldest bottles in an Alsatian winegrower's cellar are not Riesling, which they value more highly, but Pinot Gris. It takes on added depths for upward of twenty years.

On the other hand, Pinot Gris is not an assertive wine. It typically spends no time in small oak barrels, unlike many Chardonnays. Its flavor is neither especially stony nor flagrantly fruity. Rather, it tastes lush—if that could be called a taste. Pinot Gris is as much a sensation as a wine. Its strong yet accommodating character makes it perhaps the ideal wine for one of the trickiest foods of all: fresh salmon. Since I live in Oregon, I think that I have some ability to hold forth on the subject of salmon. It's so strongly flavored that it gives the back of a fin to seemingly any wine that comes its way. Curiously, most Chardonnays don't marry well with salmon. At best, it's a standoff. They don't hurt each other. A few dry Rieslings can work pretty well, but the ticket that gets stamped every time is Pinot Gris. It can be strong enough to stand up to the oily richness and pronounced flavor of the fish without getting in its way. I recommend it unreservedly.

Another specialty with Pinot Gris, something admittedly not to everyone's taste, is shad roe. Here we have richness allied with blandness, which is why rashers of bacon always hit the spot when served alongside shad roe. Yet shad roe has a real appeal, no more so than when it is served with a mature Pinot Gris. It works better than any other dry or rich white wine for this shad roe lover, although certain light red wines served cool, like Sancerre rouge, do very nicely indeed.

Unlike Pinot Gris, which is an accommodating variety, wines with assertive flavors can be difficult. Gewurztraminer is one such wine. The best examples, the Alsatian Gewurztraminers, can be so floral and spicy that they seem to roll over virtually everything in their path. This is not true, but the Gewurztraminer fan can be tempted to conclude this.

In Alsace, Gewurztraminer typically is served either as an aperitif or—and this is inspired—as an accompaniment to the local *fois gras*. Now *there* is a food that doesn't take no for an answer! But the range of Gewurztraminer extends beyond this. For some odd reason, it goes especially well with onions, don't ask me why. Gewurztraminer and onion soup is a lovely pairing, as is Gewurztraminer with any of a number of variations on the onion tarts so beloved in the region.

A less well known combination but one that works wonderfully well is the combination of a good Gewurztraminer with one of the best—and easiest—soups I know, Butternut Squash Soup. The undertone of sweetness in the squash is knifed by the spiciness of the Gewurztraminer. See for yourself.

BUTTERNUT SQUASH SOUP

Slice a small butternut squash lengthwise and scoop out the seeds. Slice into chunks for easy handling. Steam the squash until tender, about 20 minutes. Scoop the squash from the rind. Discard the rind and purée the cooked squash in a food processor or blender. Place the purée in a heavy-bottomed saucepan and add to it 2 cups of chicken stock (a can of chicken broth will do nicely), 1 tablespoon of very finely grated onion, and salt and black pepper to taste. Bring this to a boil. In the meantime, combine 2 egg yolks with 1 cup of heavy whipping cream and whisk to blend. When the soup is boiling, add the cream mixture and whisk constantly until the soup has thickened. Serve when you like. The soup will keep refrigerated for days. Serve hot, with homemade croutons on top.

Other wines can be difficult to pair because of a certain extremity of character. The best example I know of this is one of my favorite dry white wines of all, the 100 percent Chenin Blanc Loire wine called Clos de la Coulée de Serrant, which is the finest vineyard (17.3 acres) in the district of Savennières.

I have a passion for this wine which, I must confess, my wife does not share. For her, Coulée de Serrant is just too stony, too minerally, so much so that it seems feculent. It's true that when young, all of the wines of the Savennières district are unpleasantly lean and acidic. They need upward of ten years in the bottle before unbending. Then they present a whiff of honeysuckle. But the wines always remain lean, tight, and somehow severe. But few wines offer more *gout de terroir*— taste of the soil—than Savennières and none more so than Coulée de Serrant. But it's a prickly customer with food. What works? The best combination tried so far—even my wife enjoyed it—is smoked trout with a shallot-infused mayonnaise. Unlike salmon, trout is not an oily fish, so the demand for richness is not insistent. But it is a delicate flavor and it needs something to set it off. Savennières is the ticket. A mature Chablis, which is barely, if at all, less minerally than Savennières, is similarly enhancing.

As for Sauvignon Blanc, also known as Fumé Blanc, I have a confession to make: I don't care much for it. Wine writers, like disk jockeys, are never supposed to say that they don't like a wine or a song. But honesty propels me forward. I find too many Sauvignon Blancs aggressively weedy and vegetal. With food they can have the subtlety of a jackhammer. That said, I *have* tasted some Sauvignon Blancs that I've liked, particularly from the Loire districts of Sancerre and Chavignol, where they seemed to have mowed down the weediness. And I have had a few white Graves that exert an appeal, none more so than Château Laville Haut-Brion.

The reason I am so fond of Château Laville Haut-Brion is that it is preponderantly Semillon (60 percent) rather than Sauvignon Blanc (40 percent). And Semillon is a white grape of immense character when grown in the right soils. It also ages to a far finer end than Sauvignon Blanc, as well as offering a finer, more supple texture. No Sauvignon Blanc wine should leave home without it. On its own, Semillon can be a wonder, as anyone who has tasted a fifteen-year-old Australian Semillon from the Hunter Valley can happily attest. The usual description is lanolin, which is oddly evocative as pure lanolin has no scent. Yet somehow most folks know what the description implies. Semillon also is the backbone of all the great Sauternes. Some excellent Semillon now is being produced in Washington State; it's a little herbaceous at first but with age that disappears. (The same cannot be said, so far, for Washington Sauvignon Blancs, which are so vegetal that if you put a drop of motor oil in the glass and took a sniff you'd swear that a lawnmower had just passed by.)

When Semillon is given some bottle age, say five years or more, it can stand in for many Chardonnays in terms of pleasure and refinement. The immensely flavorful Australian Semillons—preposterously labeled Hunter Valley Riesling in that district—are knockouts at the dinner table, in the best sense of the term. To see just how impressive a well-aged Semillon can be, you need only try it with a dish that, admittedly, shows off any number of wines, red or white. But it does go beautifully with well-aged Semillons and—dare I say it?—the best Sauvignon Blancs.

CHICKEN BREASTS WITH GORGONZOLA AND CHIVES

PER PERSON: Place a boned chicken breast between two sheets of waxed paper and flatten slightly. Dredge the flattened chicken breast in flour generously seasoned with black pepper and salt, knocking off the excess flour. Melt 1 tablespoon of unsalted butter in a sauté pan placed over medium-high heat. Sauté the chicken breast for 2 to 3 minutes on each side, depending upon thickness. Then remove the chicken breast to a plate and place in a 250-degree oven to keep warm.

Place the sauté pan over high heat and add to it ¼ cup heavy whipping cream and 2 tablespoons dry white wine. Stir to blend. Toss in 1 teaspoon finely chopped shallots. Bring the cream to a boil and let boil, uncovered, to reduce the mixture by approximately half. Add 2 table-spoons of Gorgonzola (or other blue cheese) in small pieces and whisk it into the sauce. Continue reducing over high heat until the sauce is thick but still fluid. If it becomes overly thick, thin it with a few teaspoons of milk, cream, or wine and reduce again as needed.

Place the reserved chicken breast on a warm dinner plate and spoon the cream sauce over it. Garnish with finely snipped fresh chives or, if they are not in season, finely snipped green onion (scallion) tops. Serve with rice alongside.

The preceding dish works so well with so many wines because of the cheese in the sauce. The alliance between wine and cheese is the most famous of all. Traditionally and to this day, the usual approach in a fine French or Italian meal is to serve the finest red wine of the meal with the cheese course. At the risk of calling the gods down upon my head, I would like to differ: White wines seem to enhance many cheeses far better than reds. Clearly, the variety of cheeses is so vast that the exceptions can riddle such a generalization like the holes in yesterday's excuse. Nevertheless, I can only go by what my experience suggests.

The difficulty with cheese and many red wines—and I say this as someone who prefers reds to whites—is that they tend to overwhelm the more delicate cheeses. The sheer fruiti-ness of many red wines is the undoing of a cheese tray. A ripe brie, the real kind made from unpasteurized milk, comes alive when tasted against the backdrop of a flinty Sancerre or one of the more restrained white Burgundies such as Pernand-Vergelesses. This is not to say that no red wine partners it with suitable deference: The lighter red Bordeaux from Graves or a well-aged Chinon from the Loire are admirable.

But many cheeses, especially creamy ones, call for the cutting acidity and more obvious mineraliness of white wines. A mature Chablis, especially a *premier* or *grand cru*, is an illuminating experience. It can make a cheese come alive. Grander yet is a wine such as Chevalier-Montrachet, the great white Burgundy that often outshines its neighboring namesake Le Montrachet. It differs from its contiguous neighbor in displaying a more intense stoniness coupled with some spiciness. The role of spiciness is not to be discounted. Here Gewurztraminer, that troublesome grape, again comes into its own. Against the backdrop of some strongly flavored cheeses, notably the Alsatian specialty Munster, the once belligerent Gewurztraminer takes on a soothing quality. One of the great Alsatian restaurants, Moulin du Kaegy in Steinbrunn-le-Bas near Mulhouse, is so convinced of the superiority of Gewurztraminer with the local cheeses that an excellent bottle always accompanies the cheese tray. And the chef makes his case in the best way possible: You can taste for yourself.

Desserts present a different problem. The French like to serve Champagne, which reflects a taste for celebration as much as anything else. Yet sparkling wines do have their place. One of the most pleasurable combinations is that of Asti Spumante with chocolate. According to some, chocolate deadens the palate and is not to be advised for "serious" wine drinking. Who comes up with this stuff? One of the great food and wine combinations is chocolate with Pinot Noir. Granted, I'm not likely to haul out a bottle of La Tâche to go with a chocolate bar (it does taste pretty good, though) but few sensations are more complementary than mingling the delectable fruit of a good Pinot Noir with that of a well-made piece of bittersweet dark chocolate. Milk chocolate doesn't seem to work quite as well. Another stunning chocolate and red wine combination is bittersweet chocolate with Recioto della Valpolicella, either the dry, or *amarone*, style or the less seen but wonderful sweet, or *amabile*, version. Port also is swell, as are the fortified Muscats from Australia.

But back to Asti Spumante. Because so much of the stuff is produced—upward of seventy million bottles annually—wine snoots tend to dismiss it out of hand. Granted, a lot of what's around is second rate. But at its best, Asti Spumante is one of the world's great wines. The Asti district of the Piedmont region manages to create White Muscat grapes that have intense yet delicate flavor coupled with high acidity. You don't suspect how much acidity until you try a good Asti—whether the *spumante*, or foaming, version or the rarer *frizzante*, or prickling, version—with something as intensely chocolatey as chocolate truffles. Try an Asti Spumante from a producer such as Fontanafredda, Felice Bonardi, or Bera with this wonderfully simple version of chocolate truffles, which is all the more surprising as it was a signature creation of the late Fernand Point, who made La Pyramide the greatest restaurant in France in the 1930s, 1940s, and 1950s.

CHOCOLATE TRUFFLES FERNAND POINT

To make one dozen walnut-sized truffles: Melt 4 ounces of good bittersweet chocolate over very low heat in a small, heavy-bottomed saucepan or in the top half of a double boiler set over barely simmering water. When the chocolate is melted, stir in 3 ounces of unsalted butter, cut into small pieces. When the butter is melted and combined with the chocolate, stir in 1 tablespoon of lukewarm water. Stir to blend. Remove the chocolate from the heat. When it has cooled but still is liquid, stir in 1 egg yolk. Cover and place the saucepan in the refrigerator for the chocolate to chill and harden.

After the chocolate has hardened completely—overnight is best—remove from the refrigerator. Lay out a sheet of waxed paper. Using a butter knife, carve out walnut-sized chunks of chocolate from the saucepan and squeeze each chunk with your hand to shape it into a rough ball. The warmth of your hand, along with the pressure, will do the trick. Place the formed truffles on the waxed paper.

Push a small quantity of unsweetened cocoa powder through a fine-meshed sieve placed over a dinner plate.

It's best to be generous, as the remaining cocoa powder can be returned to the container for later use. Cover your fingertips with the powder. Then roll each truffle in the cocoa, taking care to fill in all the crevices. Place the finished truffle on a serving plate and return to the refrigerator for rehardening and chilling. Serve within 24 hours if possible.

The most famous category of dessert wines, French Sauternes and German Beerenausleses (abbreviated to BA) and Trockenbeerenausleses (TBA), are a subject unto themselves. The reason for this is that both wines, along with others like them from California, Italy, and Australia, are infused with the flavor of *Botrytis cinerea*, or "noble rot." What makes this rot noble and all the other kinds ignoble is that this form of fungus occurs late in the year. More to the point, it shrivels the grape—they do look rotten—concentrating the flavor by helping evaporate the water in the grape berry through microscopic pores bored by the fungus in the grape skin. But the fungus also imparts its own distinctive taste, which might be described as spicy/cinnamon-y. The more botrytis is found in the vineyard—it differs from year to year and even from cluster to cluster—the more pronounced the flavor and liquorous the wine.

The great Sauternes and German Rieslings of the richest sort, the BAs and TBAs, always are loaded with the botrytis taste. This despite the fact that the wines are very different in taste, Sauternes being made from Semillon and Sauvignon Blanc and boasting fourteen percent alcohol, while the German wines, typically 100 percent Riesling, are never more than 10 percent alcohol. But the botrytis taste is unmistakable. It is also assertive, lingering, and memorable.

The usual response to these wines is to suggest that they be served as desserts unto themselves. This is a mistake. The mark of a truly fine wine is that it exalts, and is exalted by, some kind of food. The choice may not be vast, but a wine that can't be uplifted by food is suspect. As has already been cited, Sauternes can earn their keep and taste better for being served with *foie gras* or Roquefort, to say nothing of oysters. (Yes, it does work.) German Riesling of the Beerenauslese level and TBA are similarly pleasurable.

This is not to say that these wines should not be served with dessert, only that it is an injustice to palate and wine to serve them *as* dessert. Because they are so striking, they need a flavorful but less assertive partner. Two desserts have proved world-beaters for this role: a richer-than-usual bread pudding devised by the Coach House restaurant in New York and one of the most ancient recipes still in use in the modern repertoire, blanc-manger.

THE COACH HOUSE BREAD PUDDING

FOR A 2-QUART BAKING DISH: Preheat the oven to 375 degrees Fahrenheit. Using 12 thin slices of good bread with the crusts removed, brush just one side of each slice lightly with melted butter. Set aside. Whisk together until completely blended 5 whole eggs, 4 egg yolks, 1 cup sugar, 4 cups (1 quart) milk, 1 cup heavy cream, 1 teaspoon vanilla extract, and a pinch of salt.

Place the bread slices, buttered side up, in the baking dish. Pour the milk mixture through a fine-meshed strainer over the bread slices. Bake the bread pudding at 375 degrees for 45 minutes or until a knife or skewer plunged into the center of the pudding comes out clean. Just before serving, sprinkle the pudding with a generous amount of confectioners' sugar and glaze the bread pudding by running it under the broiler.

The name of blanc-manger comes from the Old French, to eat white. It used to be the exclusive fare of the upper class, by virtue of the amount of labor once required to make the dish, which calls for almond milk which used to have to be extracted by pounding almonds laboriously in a mortar and pestle and adding water to extract the milky white exudation. The food processor has changed all that. This is one of the most sublime and delicate desserts possible.

BLANC-MANGER

FOR A 1-QUART MOLD: Toss 12 ounces of raw, unsalted, unblanched whole almonds into boiling water for 1 minute to loosen the skins. Drain immediately. Then remove the skins by pinching the almonds between your fingers. The almond will fly off like a bullet, leaving you holding the skin the way some reptiles elude their predators. No matter. Capture the skinned almonds in a bowl and discard the skins.

Place the almonds in a food processor and process until small chunks are created. With the processor going, pour 2 cups of cold water into the chopped almonds. Continue processing briefly. The liquid will be milky white.

Line a colander with two thicknesses of well-washed cheesecloth with ample lengths draping over the sides and place it over a large mixing bowl. Pour the contents of the food processor into the lined colander and let drain. Then twist the cheesecloth to completely and tightly enclose the chopped almonds and twist to extract the ample remaining liquid. This is an important step, as much flavor is retained in this undrained liquid. Discard the now-dry chopped almonds, as their flavor has been extracted. You should have nearly 2 cups of almond milk in the bowl. Set aside.

In a small saucepan, sprinkle 1½ envelopes of unflavored granulated gelatin in ¼ cup cold water. Place over very low heat and stir continuously for several minutes until the gelatin dissolves. Then add the gelatin to the almond milk, along with 1 cup heavy cream and ½ cup sugar.

Whisk to blend and then transfer the mixture to a heavy-bottomed saucepan. Bring the mixture nearly, but not quite, to a boil, whisking frequently to dissolve the sugar and blend the gelatin. When it approaches the boiling point, remove from heat. Set aside and let cool completely.

Oil the mold lightly with almond oil or a flavorless oil like cottonseed oil (Wesson, for example). Pour the completely cooled blanc-manger into the oiled mold and refrigerate for 4 hours or more. To serve, run a thin knife around the perimeter of the blanc-manger and invert over a lightly moistened presentation plate. (The moistening will let you slide the blanc-manger into the center of the plate if you're not quite bull's eye on the landing.) If it refuses to unmold, jostle it a bit.

Blanc-manger frequently is flavored with various liqueurs or *eaux-de-vie* such as kirsch. If you wish to do this—which is undesirable if a fine wine is being served alongside—add 2 tablespoons after the blanc-manger has cooled but before it is poured into the mold. Blanc-manger often is served, with great effect, with whatever fresh fruit is in season.

RED WINES

Choosing red wines to pair with foods is, curiously, easier than choosing whites. This probably has to do with the fact that most red wines are more overtly flavorful than most white wines. The result is that they can be served interchangeably with any number of red meats, sausages, or the like. This is not to say that some red wines, such as Barolo or Hermitage, don't go with certain foods or dishes better than, say, Beaujolais or Chinon.

Choosing wines can be likened to coming up with a strategy in squash, racquetball, or handball, where you have a four-wall game. You can play a side-wall game, in which you make as many shots as possible along the side walls. Or you can play short or long, dropping your shots close to the front wall or far to the rear. Good players mix it up and keep less skilled players like myself running in a bewildered daze until we drop. But it is stimulating.

The wine version of this is viewing wines in terms of rusticity and refinement; delicacy and robustness; fruity youth or ethereal age; and so on. This makes more sense, at least in helping to decide what goes with what, than looking only at grape variety or even district. In a well-orchestrated dinner, as in a squash game, you can't go for put-away shots too often. So it is with wine. Too many grand wines in one sitting are not only boring, but deadening.

From this perspective, consider Barbera, one of the most underrated red wines—and grape varieties—in the world. Although grown in California, the finest versions come from Italy, none better than those labeled Barbera d'Alba in the Piedmont region. There, producers such as Vietti, Prunotto, Aldo Conterno, Giacomo Conterno, Paolo Scavino, Angelo Gaja, Bruno Giacosa, and Riccardo Fennochio, among others, are reinvigorating a wine that too often has been dismissed as unworthy of attention. Is it as fine as Nebbiolo, the grape of Barolo and Barbaresco? No, it isn't. But without the backdrop of Barbera preceding these wines in a meal, the tremendous breed of Nebbiolo is less readily apparent. And without Barolo and Barbaresco, the essential rusticity of Barbera is not always so recognizable either, especially now when it is so carefully grown and painstakingly vinified by the producers mentioned previously. And even more so when a good Barbera takes on ten years or so of age and its exuberant, almost raw fruitiness defers to more modulated but complete flavors and scents. Then it takes its place in the long game.

You can play Barbera in the short game of youthful fruitiness. It is drinkable young, popping with a bright burst of fruit enlivened by the high acidity that makes this wine so refreshing. Here the natural ally is something rich or respectably greasy, like a good sausage. Pâté is a good choice, especially a coarse-textured country pâté with its characteristic chunks of fat. One of the best country pâté recipes I know is the following French pâté, which, nationalities aside, goes extremely well with Barbera.

A FRENCH COUNTRY PÂTÉ

FOR A 10-CUP LOAF PAN: Preheat the oven to 400 degrees Fahrenheit. Have ready a larger pan in which the loaf pan will fit and that can hold water halfway up the sides of the loaf pan to create a *bain-marie*. Have sufficient water ready at the boil to create the hot-water bath when needed.

Using a food processor (or a meat grinder), process to a medium-coarse texture 1 pound of boneless pork shoulder, 1 pound of boneless veal of a cheap cut, and ¾ pound fresh pork fat, preferably from the loin. If you're using a food processor, it's a good idea to process the pork fat first to the desired texture and add it to the ground meat later on. Process the meats together in small portions at a time to ensure an even consistency of texture. Set aside.

Purée together 1 pound of chicken livers, 6 cloves of peeled garlic, 3 eggs, ¼ cup heavy cream, and ½ cup of brandy. With the purée still in the food processor, add to it about one-third of the meat mixture and process briefly to combine. Then add to it 3 teaspoons of salt, 2 teaspoons freshly ground black pepper, ½ teaspoon ground allspice, and ½ teaspoon ground cinnamon. Process briefly again to blend the seasonings into the meat mixture.

Pour the contents of the food processor into a large mixing bowl. Add to it the remaining meat mixture. Using your hands, combine the mixtures thoroughly. Then add to it ½ cup flour and mix thoroughly again to combine. Line the bottom and sides of the 10-cup loaf pan with thickly sliced bacon. You'll need ¾ pound to 1 pound of bacon depending upon the thickness of the slices. Reserve several slices for the top. Use only one layer of bacon.

Pour the pâté mixture into the bacon-lined pan, patting the mixture to eliminate air holes. Place one layer of bacon strips on top. Cover tightly with a double thickness of aluminum foil. Place the loaf pan inside the *bain-marie* and pour in enough water to come halfway up the sides of the loaf pan. Bake in the preheated oven for 3 hours. Then remove the aluminum foil and bake for another 15 minutes or so to allow the top strips of bacon to brown.

Remove from the oven, but do not pour off the juices. Place the pan on a baking sheet with raised sides to catch overflowing juices and then weight it with a foil-wrapped brick or use another loaf pan filled with tin cans or rice. This will compress the pâté and make for easier slicing. Let cool completely and then remove the weight. Serve at room temperature. The pâté will keep and improve for up to 10 days in the refrigerator.

A pâté like this will pair beautifully with any number of red wines, even something as refined as Château Lafite-Rothschild. (I tried it once and neither wine nor pâté came off the worse for it.) Nevertheless, the short game of fruitiness and rusticity works best. Almost any young Cabernet Sauvignon will serve, although the lighter-weight fruit and higher acidity of the Cabernet Franc that creates Chinon and Bourgueil from the Loire Valley works even better.

High acidity helps with country pâté. Young Chianti is ideal, as is Côtes du Rhône, Buzet from southwest France, and Minervois and Corbières from the Midi region of France near Nîmes. All sorts of young red Bordeaux work admirably, as well as any of Italy's innumerable rustic reds such as Montepulciano d'Abruzzo, Refosco from Friuli, various red wines made from the ancient Aglianico grape such as Falerno, Irpinia Rosso, and Taurasi, the last two wines being specialities of the great producer Mastroberardino. The Italian list is too long to be enumerated. Not to be forgotten is California Zinfandel, providing that the wines are not so overripe—a common ailment—as to make them flabby or lacking in acidity. But the best are terrific accompaniments.

The wines mentioned previously are not considered "serious" wines. (This is an awkward phrase. The Italians do it much better, calling a really fine wine *vino da meditazione*, a wine to meditate over.) A stimulating twist would be to serve a country pâté with a wine worth meditating over. This is the equivalent of setting up your opponent for a hard shot to the back court only to drop it in softly in the front. They can't help but grin when they see the result. The same is true of serving country pâté with something as grand as a great red Bordeaux like Château Mouton-Rothschild or Château Pétrus, both of which can look the better against the backdrop of such simple yet flavorful fare. Alternatively, a Côte-Rotie or Hermitage would be ideal, muscular yet profound as they are. Not to be forgotten are Barolo or Barbaresco, to say nothing of great red Burgundies. This business of grand with humble is not a table version of social affectation, like bringing home a hobo in a 1930s scavenger hunt. Here it's a way of adding a sharper edge to the wine, the food, and, not least, to your own increased awareness of both. It makes you sit up.

Great red wines, by virtue of the storm of sensations they carry, call for restraint on the part of those fortunate enough to serve them. The problem is that too often it seems that the host feels compelled to offer a correspondingly grand dish, usually something very French, very *haute*, and very rich. It's a rare red wine that is the better for this experience, to say nothing of the diner. Sensory overload appears to be the problem.

This is not to say that a diet of water crackers and steak tartare is called for, but rather, something not overly elaborate. A good example of this would be a well-aged saddle of lamb. I mention well-aged—which somehow sounds more appropriate to wine than to lamb—because a fair amount of personal trial and (delicious) error in tasting saddles of lamb aged varying lengths of time has led to the conclusion that, as with fine wine, a transformation occurs over time with lamb that is devoutly to be wished. I like lamb immensely and I'll happily eat it without aging if that's how it's served. But the best cut is the saddle and when hung in a proper meat locker, where the temperature and humidity are controlled, it takes on new dimensions. Tastes in the matter of hanging beef or lamb vary, but I've found that between three and four weeks is ideal. Less than that and the transformation is minimal. More than that and it takes on, to me anyway, a gamey quality that overrides the pungently sweet flavor of lamb. At three to four weeks of age, this flavor seems at its fullest and most rewarding.

The only trick to serving such lamb is the foresight to order it from a reputable butcher sufficiently ahead of time. What you want is a saddle of lamb dry-aged for three to four weeks. Nowadays, much of the meat delivered to a butcher already is divided into so-called primal cuts. These are tightly wrapped in a vacuum-sealed plastic called Cryovac. Because all of the moisture is retained in a Cryovac bag, meat will not age properly in one. Instead, it must be removed and hung on a hook open to the cold, moist air of a meat locker. There it will slowly lose moisture and become more dense, as well as undergo the autolysis process whereby enzymes in the meat tenderize the fibers and impart a flavor, which compensates for the moisture loss by making the meat more tender.

Although this will offend purists, the best thing to do is order two saddles of lamb to be aged for three to four weeks, eat one and freeze the other. Lamb, like beef, freezes well and if the freezer is zero degrees or less, it will keep for months.

A SIMPLE ROAST SADDLE OF LAMB

TO SERVE SIX PEOPLE: Have the butcher bone out the saddle of lamb, remove all but ⅛ inch to ¼ inch of the fat and roll and tie it. This makes it far easier to slice and results in no loss of succulence, no matter what purists might say. A 3½-pound saddle will take about 45 minutes roasting time; a 4½-pound saddle requires 55 minutes. An additional 10 minutes "resting time" outside the oven after roasting should be added to allow the juices to recede into the meat.

Preheat the oven to 450 degrees. Slice 4 to 6 large cloves of peeled garlic into slivers and, after making small incisions in various points along the roll, push the garlic slivers into the meat. Season lightly with salt, freshly ground black pepper (not too much), and crumbled dried rosemary. Press these onto the fat on all sides. Place the meat on a roasting rack and set in the middle of the oven. Roast at 450 degrees for 15 minutes and then lower the heat to 400 degrees and continue roasting for another 30 minutes.

When the internal temperature reads 140 degrees, the lamb will be medium-rare, the meat pinkish in the interior but not rosy red. An instant-reading thermometer is the ticket here. Let the roast rest for 10 minutes and then snip off the ties and slice crosswise into 1-inch-thick slices. Serve these on very warm plates, accompanied by scalloped potatoes, the French version called *gratin Dauphinois* or the exceedingly good version of creamed potatoes, below, from Lapérouse restaurant in Paris.

CREAMED POTATOES LAPÉROUSE

TO SERVE 6 PEOPLE: Peel about 3 pounds of waxy-type potatoes. Place these in a large pot of water and bring to a boil. Let simmer until the potatoes are easily penetrated with a skewer or the point of a knife, about 20 minutes depending upon the size of the potatoes. They should not be overcooked. Drain and let cool until they can be handled. Then slice the cooked potatoes into thick slices, about ¼ inch thick. Set aside.

Bring to a boil 2 cups of milk seasoned with a large pinch of salt and freshly grated nutmeg and black pepper. When

it reaches the boil, immediately add the potato slices and
2 cups of heavy whipping cream. Let the mixture boil
for 10 minutes. The starch in the potatoes will thicken
the milk and cream. Let boil until the liquid is thickened
to taste. Before serving, stir in several pats of unsalted
butter and check for seasonings. This dish can be prepared ahead of time and gently reheated. Thin out the
liquid with additional milk or cream as needed. Serve
hot on very warm plates.

Choosing the red wine to go with this repast is a delicious agony. Since so many serve so well, you might want
to consider the preferences of your guests. If the crowd
swoons over Bordeaux, then nothing could be finer than a
majestic St.-Emilion like Château Cheval-Blanc or Château
Ausone, to say nothing of lesser lights from that abundant
district. Still within Bordeaux, almost any mature wine from
the Médoc will carry the day, from the perfumey qualities
of a Margaux to the ripeness of St.-Julien to the austerity
of St.-Estèphe. Not to be forgotten is red Graves, none
better than Château Haut-Brion or Château La Mission-
Haut-Brion, which since September 1987 are more properly
classified as wines from Pessac-Léognan, a new appellation
in the northern Graves district.

If California wine is the excitement of the audience,
then no one could contest the supremacy of Cabernet Sauvignon with the lamb, although a top-notch Zinfandel or
Syrah can make an excellent showing. But Cabernet has the
edge and in California the choices are boggling. Among the
picks must surely be Ridge, Heitz, Dunn, Caymus, Beau-
lieu, Inglenook, Clos du Val, Chappellet, Jordan, Robert
Mondavi, Louis Martini, Stag's Leap Wine Cellars, and such
brand-named, high-end bottlings as Dominus, Opus One,
and the like.

Not to be forgotten are Australian Cabernets—and
Shiraz—none better than those from the Coonawarra (aborig-

ine for "wild honeysuckle"), one of the southernmost and therefore coolest districts in Australia. It lies about 250 miles south of Adelaide. Its distinction is twofold: the climate is Bordeaux-like and the soil, iron-red on the surface, is, eighteen inches farther down, pure limestone. The result is Cabernet and Shiraz (Syrah) of exceptional finesse and discernible *gout de terroir*. Look for various bottlings by Lindemans (Pyrus, Saint George Vineyard); Mildara; Petaluma; Redman's, and Brand's Laira.

Perhaps the ideal wine, if the properly aged bottle is available and the table-mates amenable, is Barolo or Barbaresco. The high acidity of Nebbiolo, which composes these wines, seems to be made for the sweetness of lamb. The trick is a good producer and sufficient bottle age, about ten years in a good vintage. In Barolo look for Cantina Mascarello, Marcarini, Aldo Conterno, Giacomo Conterno, Vietti, Bruno Giacosa, Prunotto, Renato Ratti, and Giuseppe Mascarello. In Barbaresco the names to watch include Angelo Gaja, Castello di Neive, Bruno Giacosa, Giovannini-Moresco, Marchesi di Gresy, Produttori del Barbaresco, Prunotto, Vietti, and Le Colline.

Alternatively, nothing beats a good Burgundy, but it should be one with stuffings, i.e., from a good vintage and, of course, producer. Some of the most rewarding red Burgundies so far tried have included various red Cortons (Tollot-Beaut, Louis Jadot); Volnay (Marquis d'Angerville, Domaine de la Pousse d'Or); Gevrey-Chambertin (Leroy, Phillipe Leclerc, Joseph Roty); Vosne-Romanée (Domaine de la Romanée-Conti, Domaine Daniel Rion, Domaine Jean Grivot); and Chassagne-Montrachet (Domaine Ramonet-Prudhon, Domaine Bachelet-Ramonet).

Apart from grand red wines for grand occasions, a loving word should be put in for that legion of red wines that can uplift an everyday moment into something that lingers in the mind. For example, one of my favorite recollections is taking a Burgundian friend who was visiting us in Oregon to the Oregon coast, which is rightly famous for its spectacular scenery. I made one of the simplest and most gratifying picnic lunches I know, the Provençal sandwich called *pan bagnat*, literally, "bathed bread." It consists of a good-sized section of crusty French or Italian bread (a small, whole round loaf is best) sliced lengthwise, most of the crumb removed, and the interior doused with good olive oil. The sandwich is composed of a variety of ingredients, as your larder takes you, but the best versions include anchovies, sliced hard-cooked eggs, tuna, and sliced tomatoes and onions. It's best if the sandwich sits for a bit to let the flavors commingle.

Any number of red wines would have been terrific. I happened to choose Dolcetto, a red wine (and grape variety) from the Piedmont. It has the necessary acidity and forthrightness of flavor to accompany a mouthful like *pan bagnat*. Dolcetto is a foot soldier in the legion of red wines that do daily service. These wines usually fail to get their due, if only because they don't cost too much and the quantities are always substantial.

Another example of such a dish would be the classic Tuscan bean dish in which Great Northern or Cannellini beans are soaked overnight, drained, and then gently simmered for one and a half or two hours, seasoned lightly with salt, pepper, and maybe a bit of crumbled rosemary, and then annointed with extra-virgin olive oil while the beans are still warm. The fragrance is heavenly. With a dish like this you could serve anything: Chianti, of course; Valpolicella; Minervois; Zinfandel; Shiraz; Côtes-du-Rhône; a basic Merlot; Spanish Tempranillo wines; Portuguese reds from the Bairrada district; Corbières; cru Bourgeois Bordeaux; or Barbera.

These wines should be served cool, in generous quantity, accompanied by nothing more than grunts of satisfaction and satiation. What results is the reverse of the old line about how "I forget the girl, I forget the place, but the wine was Chambertin." Here the moment is bright in the mind and so, too, is the taste—if not the name—of the wine.

Bibliography

Allen, Warner H. *A History of Wine*. New York: Horizon, 1961.

———. *The Romance of Wine*. New York: Dutton, 1932.

Amerine, Maynard A. "Flavor as a Value," in *Food and Civilization, A Symposium*. Springfield, Ill.: Charles Thomas, 1968.

Austin, Cedric. *The Science of Wine*. New York: American Elsevier, 1968.

Berlyne, D. E. "The Influence of Complexity and Novelty in Visual Figures on Orienting Response," *Journal of Experimental Psychology*, 55, 1958, pp. 289–295.

Berry, Charles Walter. *In Search of Wine—A Tour of the Vineyards of France*. London: Constable, 1935.

Braudel, Fernand. *Civilization and Capitalism, 15th–18th Century*, Vols. I, II, III. New York: Harper & Row, 1982–1984.

Busby, James. *Journal of a Tour*. Sydney: 1833; Hunter's Hill NSW facsimile reprint 1979 David Ell Press.

————. *A Treatise on the Culture of the Vine and the Art of Making Wine*. Australia: 1825; Hunter's Hill facsimile reprint 1979 David Ell Press.

Conant, James Bryant, ed. *Harvard Case Histories in Experimental Science*, Volume II. Cambridge, Mass.: Harvard University Press, 1964.

Cuny, Hilaire. *Louis Pasteur—The Man and His Theories*, trans. Patrick Evans. Paul S. Ericksson, 1966.

Dember, W. N.; R. W. Earl; and N. Paradise. "Response by Rats to Differential Stimulus Complexity," *Journal of Comparative Physiology and Psychology*, 50, 1957, pp. 514–518.

Doty, Richard L., ed. "Smell Identification Ability: Changes With Age," *Science*, December 21, 1984, pp. 1441–1442.

Escudier, Jean-Noël. *The Wonderful Food of Provence*, trans. Peta J. Fuller. Boston: Houghton Mifflin, 1968.

Faith, Nicholas. "A Difficult Vintage," *The Economist*, December 24, 1983, pp. 3–18.

————. *The Winemasters*. New York: Harper & Row, 1978.

Forbes, Patrick. *Champagne: The Wine, the Land and the People*. London: Victor Gollancz, 1967.

Francis, Alan David. *The Wine Trade*. New York: Harper & Row, 1972.

George, Rosemary. *The Wines of Chablis and the Yonne*. London: Sotheby's, 1984.

Ginestet, Bernard. *Chablis*. Paris: Fernand Nathan, 1986.

Hanson, Anthony. *Burgundy*. London: Faber and Faber, 1982.

Haraszthy, Agoston. *Grape Culture, Wines, and Wine-Making*. New York: Harper and Brothers, 1862; facsimile reprint, Hopewell, New Jersey: Booknoll Reprints, 1971.

Holland, Bernard. "In Praise of Early Music," *The New York Times Magazine*, May 22, 1983, pp. 64, 65, 79, and 82.

Johnson, Hugh; Dora Jane Janson; and David Revere Mc-Fadden. *Wine: Celebration and Ceremony*. New York: Smithsonian/Cooper-Hewitt, 1985.

Kavanaugh, T. E.; R. N. Skinner; and B. J. Clark. "Light-Struck Flavor Formation in Beer in Illuminated Display Cabinets," *Brewers Digest*, February 1983.

Kressmann, Edouard. *The Wonder of Wine*. New York: Hastings House, 1968.

Kunkee, Ralph E. "Selection and Modification of Yeasts and Lactic Acid Bacteria for Wine Fermentation," *Food Microbiology*, January 1984, pp. 315–332.

Loubère, Leo A. *The Red and the White—The History of Wine in France and Italy in the Nineteenth Century*. Albany: State University of New York Press, 1978.

Macpherson, C.C.H. "Life on the Shelf," *Wines and Spirits*, December 1982, p. 20.

Olney, Richard. *Yquem*. Boston: David R. Godine, 1986.

Pasteur, Louis. *Études sur le Vinaigre et sur le Vin* (1866), in *Oeuvres de Pasteur Réunies, Tome III, par Pasteur Vallery-Radot*. Paris: Masson et Cie., 1922.

———. *Mémoire sur la Fermentation appelée lactique* (1857), in *Oeuvres de Pasteur Réunies, Tome II, par Pasteur Vallery-Radot*. Paris: Masson et Cie., 1922.

The Pasteur Fermentation Centennial 1857–1957, A Scientific Symposium. New York: Chas. Pfizer and Co., 1957.

Patton, William. *Bible Wines or the Laws of Fermentation and the Wines of the Ancients*. New York: National Temperance Society, 1880.

Peynaud, Emile. *Knowing and Making Wine*, 2nd ed., trans. Alan Spencer. New York: John Wiley, 1984.

Pinkerton, R. C. "Information Theory and Melody," *Scientific American*, February 1956, pp. 77–86.

Redding, Cyrus. *Every Man His Own Butler*. London: Whittaker, Treacher and Arnot, 1852.

———. *French Wines and Vineyards; And the Way to Find Them*. London: Houston and Wright, 1860.

———. *A History and Description of Modern Wines*. London: Whittaker, Treacher and Arnot, 1833.

Shand, P. Morton. *A Book of French Wines*. New York: Alfred A. Knopf, 1928.

———. *A Book of French Wines*, rev. and ed. by Cyril Ray. Middlesex, England: Penguin, 1964.

———. *A Book of Other Wines Than French*. New York: Alfred A. Knopf, 1929.

———. *A Book of Wine*. London: Guy Chapman, 1926.

Simon, André. *Bottlescrew Days—Wine Drinking in England During the Eighteenth Century*. London: Duckworth, 1926.

Singleton, Vernon L. "Aging of Wines and Other Spiritous Products Accelerated by Physical Treatments," *Hilgardia*, May 1962, pp. 319–392.

———, and Cornelius S. Ough. "Complexity of Flavor and Blending of Wines," *Journal of Food Science*, February 1962, pp. 189–196.

Stevenson, Tom. *Champagne*. London: Sotheby's, 1986.

Thudichum, John Louis William, and August Dupré. *A Treatise on the Origin, Nature and Varieties of Wine: Being a Complete Manual of Viticulture and Oenology*. New York: Macmillan, 1872.

Turner, Ben, and Paul Roycroft. *The Winemaker's Encyclopedia*. London: Faber and Faber, 1979.

Warner, Charles K. *The Winegrowers of France and the Government Since 1875*. New York: Columbia University Press, 1960.

Weber, Eugen. *Peasants into Frenchmen—The Modernization of Rural France 1870–1914*. Palo Alto, Calif.: Stanford University Press, 1976.

Younger, William. *Gods, Men and Wine*. Cleveland, Ohio: Wine and Food Society/World, 1966.

Zeldin, Theodore. *France 1848–1945*, Vols. I and II. London: Oxford University Press, 1977.

Index